Visual Forms
of American TV Series

DONG CHAO AND ZHANG JIARUI

author**HOUSE**®

AuthorHouse™
1663 Liberty Drive
Bloomington, IN 47403
www.authorhouse.com
Phone: 833-262-8899

Published by AuthorHouse 06/24/2023

ISBN: 979-8-8230-1077-1 (sc)
ISBN: 979-8-8230-1078-8 (e)

Library of Congress Control Number: 2023911579

CATALOGUE

VISUAL FORMS OF AMERICAN TV SERIES

1. Video is a transcendent art of visual reception. Through the acceptance of the visual form by the eyeballs, the image matches one's own cognitive experience, and finally achieves the completion of acceptance and understanding. The essence of images is an extension of the senses. Today's era is dominated by flat images. It has been a hundred years since the birth of movies to the activity of self-media. In essence, this is not the final form, but A transitional state of human-to-human scene communication, this transitional state is the possibility of maximizing approaching scene interaction under the current technical means. There are mainly two parts, listening and watching, between the image and the receiver. It is the sensory amplification of the sensory organs that people receive external stimuli. With the continuous enhancement of sensory experience, with the advancement of human technology, this enhancement is gradually approaching presence, that is, sceneization. The possibility of 5G and holographic images just illustrates this problem. This chapter does not discuss the resultant relationship between audio-visual, because in the practice of image communication, the importance of viewing is far greater than that of listening to the audience, or in other words, viewing is more important than the cooperation of listening to the audience. Therefore, this chapter mainly discusses the content of visual arts.

Visual art is a seen image. It may be the simplest and more powerful if all art is taken care of from the perspective of form. The reason why formalist aesthetics lasts forever lies in its relatively hard and objective starting point. Visual art is a kind of seen image, which is mainly completed through seeing, that is to say, there are at least three aspects of thinking. The part that the communicator needs to consider, secondly, for the recipient, being able to see what is an important fulcrum that stimulates aesthetic feelings, and finally the uncertainty between transmission and reception due to objective changes in time and space just gives This spread introduces relative uncertainty. Therefore, seeing inspires the beauty of imagery in visual form. Form has become the main way of expressing the beauty of this image.

There are two very important elements in the process of seeing: eye movement and matching cognition. That is what we often say to see and feel. This is an important issue in the visual communication of film and television works. The research on eyeball movement is mainly concentrated in the field of brain science. In the known brain science of human beings, the research on the relationship between eye and brain has been quite rich, but all the research is focused on the single binary opposition of "stimulus response". In 1992, Damasio, a famous American neuroscientist, not only broke the dualism of mind and body for the first time in his famous book "The Error of Descartes", but also proved the feeling beyond the stimulus response with an unconfirmable proof process. And feeling or mental activity also comes from sensory stimulation. In other words, he used brain science to prove that aesthetics comes from the objective in natural science, and unified the subjective and objective theories for the first time at the philosophical level. Therefore, the seeing part of eye movement has become an important part of the visual aesthetics of film and television works. Form, as a kind of external rhythm, internal feeling, and flow concept of internal and external unity, plays an important role in the stimulation of eye movement. Through seeing—an extension of the visual sense, the audience sees a man-made image "spectacle" beyond the experience world. Human senses have a fixed threshold, and the eyes' capture of color must strictly abide by Sir Newton's color law of light Yes, the human ear is also clearly in a hertz frequency band, as are other senses, so film and television works give a possibility of transcending sensory experience, and this transcendence in form is mainly reflected in extreme and unrealistic combinations. First of all, the so-called extreme refers to the use of angles, perspectives, scenes, colors, light, etc. in film and television works, or in visual forms. For example, it is difficult for us to keep getting close to a person's face in normal life. In the world, I feel the visual experience of close-up scenes without talking, but it can be presented in film and television works. For example, it is difficult for us to achieve God's perspective all the time, that is, overlooking an area, but the current lens can often be viewed from a bird's-eye view. An area to be photographed, for example, it is difficult for us to see the combination of extremely beautiful lights and colors in real life, but we can often see it in film and television dramas, so if the extreme visual form is an artistic technique, It is better to say that the visual form presents a transcendence of real life, a kind of sensory transcendence. The current human technology level can achieve sensory transcendence. Visual art is the furthest, surpassing life and experience. In the film and television works, we continue to use the real experience world as the blueprint, so that the audience can see the extremism of the experience world. In fact, in the portrayal of the extreme visual form of the film and television works, it serves to transcend the experience of the world. We I have imagined a lot, but the dimensionality has been reduced to the world we are familiar with. Secondly, unrealistic combination refers to the transcendence of feelings based on the real world, that is, the random splicing between pictures, the random splicing of the recipient's self-feeling, the random splicing of the process of transmission and reception, and the purpose of each connection is to Based on transcending reality, although it sounds like non-linear editing or splicing of computer software, it is actually not. Video editing is a kind of image control, and it is an inevitable product in the era of low-tech production and linear communication. After reviewing the previous logic, according to Damasio's theory (currently no philosophical circles or brain science circles have stood up to refute his point of view, so we can accept it for the time being) feeling comes from objective stimuli, and thoughts also come from objective stimuli. Aesthetics also come from objective stimuli. Then the stimulation of all film and television works comes from the transcendence of the real sensory world, and film and television works try their best to express this transcendence in form. Zhao Tingyang, a famous philosopher of the Chinese Academy of Sciences, wrote in the book "The Fulcrum of First Philosophy": Transcendence is inevitable for human beings. This kind of philosophical judgment comes not only from the observation of reality, but also from the rebellion of people against themselves. Thought comes from the betrayal of feelings, and aesthetics comes from the transcendence of reality, accepting but not satisfied. Therefore, the unrealistic combination of film and television works referred to here refers to the possibility of objectively transcending linear time, beyond the possibility of the perceived world, and the transcendence of time based on the premise of space transcendence, or the three-dimensional people's perception of the four-dimensional The spiritual longing for life, although I will die, but the spirit will last forever, this is the life myth discourse system built by the East and the West for thousands of years, so the transcendence of visual form is the most desired demand of the audience. Unconstrained editing art, colorful lighting images, colorful scenes, and exciting story rhythms all create combination possibilities objectively and increase imagination space subjectively.

match and cognition. When it comes to acceptance, it is necessary to talk about audience research. The audience research in communication studies is overwhelming. However, in addition to the initial research on how to accept the central idea, it also mainly talks about the reasons for acceptance. After thinking about all the reasons, it is found that the reason for all acceptance is hope. Live beyond. So when the dynamic images in film and television works pour into the human brain like flowing water, the memory and recognition functions of the brain start to start. What starts in the brain is what to record, how to combine, how to store, how to express, etc. Brain Science Questions, but the most important point is that the brain will screen whether the image it sees needs to be remembered. There is a very interesting sentence in communication studies. At that time, the Palo Alto school's famous saying, as a communicator, "I can't decide how you think, but I can decide what to think." The effect of receiving is like a shot of stimulant, because this sentence opens up the possibility that the effect of communication can be constructed, but brain science breaks this optimistic prediction: acceptance comes from empirical cognition. That is to say, the premise of the deterministic communication effect is the uncertain life past, and the uncertainty accepted by individuals is an event that cannot be accurately predicted, but can be described regularly. Borrowing the famous "Schrödinger's cat" as an analogy, the communicators or agenda setters strive for the communication effect, and in the end it is "Schrödinger's cat", which cannot be determined until the last moment. What is more complicated than life and death is the fluidity of acceptance. Life and death are accurate states, while acceptance and cognition are uncertain states. What is accepted today may not be accepted tomorrow, and what is accepted tomorrow may not be accepted the day after tomorrow. It is constantly changing., and it is difficult to describe this change process. After all, human beings are not purely quantum, so the uncertainty of image acceptance can only be described relatively accurately by laws (or more accurately called a stable state at a certain time). In many reception histories, people found that with the transformation of media technology, human beings have been trying to develop hearing and vision until the later audio-visual combination. However, at the end of 4G and the early stage of 5G, the development of vision by human communicators has reached To the extreme, the deepening of visual development is actually the result of grasping the commonality of human acceptance laws. People have gradually discovered that the transcendent aesthetics of visual form is the fact that can best synthesize the largest number of audiences. Therefore, the main reason for audiences to accept art dominated by visual forms is to accept commonality, an inevitability based on sensory enhancement.

Therefore, in film and television art, the visual imagery of visual art comes from the transcendent needs of the audience and the development of visualization under the existing technical conditions. It is an important manifestation of sensory enhancement. The audience themselves internalize what they see into the perception of self-transcendence, and magnify this perception into an aesthetic image, so it is said that the visual form is a visible image.

2. In cross-cultural communication, visual forms can transcend cultural differences. This kind of acceptance mechanism has common characteristics when it is transmitted across cultures, so the visual form is the most capable of crossing cultures. As mentioned above, the visual form is a regular description derived from the general acceptance of the audience, so this universality should and must be reflected in different cultures and different nations, which is the sense of resonance mentioned by most researchers. When we examine cultural differences, we will find that the so-called cultural differences mainly come from the common historical experience of life in the cultural circle, and this life experience has accumulated many aspects such as living habits, language, cognition, and mythology. But in the final analysis, these differences can be understood as the different

ways of sensory reception and expression. Compared with other senses, the transcendence of the visual form in the communication process is the most obvious. The sensory abilities include: vision, hearing, feeling, smell, touch, taste, etc., among which the most aspects can be communicated under the existing technical conditions It is vision and hearing, that is to say, from the perspective of time and space, the sensory organs that can break the constraints of time and space are hearing and vision. Again, this judgment is based on the premise of existing communication technology, because human beings The spread of the world is evolving towards omnipotent presence, so what the current technology can achieve is the transcendence of vision and hearing. And because the previous article has proved that in the current communication environment, visual art is superior to auditory experience in terms of content diversity, audience acceptance and other dimensions, so visual art is the most capable cross-cultural art under the current situation. An art form of spreading the workhorse. Therefore, a visual art that is objectively needed, fully developed in reality, and can satisfy the audience on the basis of spiritual needs is an important art form of cross-cultural communication.

American dramas are effective in cross-cultural communication. Not only has it become a form of drama that the world is willing to accept, it has even become a new force on the cultural front. Combining the above, in analyzing the unique performance advantages of American drama cross-cultural communication, the author believes that there are the following aspects, which are important manifestations of visual forms.

① The stimulation and resonance brought by the transcendence of the rhythm combination;

The editing techniques that are often used in American dramas are: accumulating montages, high-speed editing and other methods can easily lead to a fast pace. For example, in "House of Cards", this combination is often used to express tension and stimulate the audience's perception. The transcendence of the rhythm comes from the awakening or recognition of the inner consciousness of the audience, and the stimulation and response effect is brought about by the contrast. In cross-cultural communication, this rhythm is the most capable of breaking through language and cultural barriers. Humans have basically the same response to perception.

Eastern audiences and Western audiences may have different cultural understandings of the film, but they share the same perception of basic emotions and cognitive stimuli. For example, in the movie "Harry Potter", the Western audience's understanding of the protagonist's hair color can be clarified, but the Eastern audience's understanding of this culture is not accurate due to the lack of this cultural gene. Orientals do not have black hair Represents the Romans, white hair represents the Germans, red hair represents the Celts, and the genetic ability to distinguish races based on hair color, but can be analyzed based on the visual language used in the film, the basic identity of common emotions and plot promotion are both Interpretation of the film can be completed.

At the beginning of the production of American dramas, the target of broadcasting is set to the whole world, that is to say, its production purpose is as global as that of Hollywood. The global production purpose will inevitably bring pan-cultural identity attributes in the production process. In terms of combination, in addition to the most basic film and television combination method, a combination method that can be positive to the audience has also been added. Therefore, purpose is very important. In American dramas such as "Breaking Bad", the fast-paced, transcendent combination is the rhythm feature throughout the entire TV series. Similarly, a transcendent narrative method is also used in the combination of the plots. For example, in the narrative mode, the first impression that American TV dramas give the audience is "unexpected". This unexpected feeling mainly comes from the contrast of the combination of narratives. Narrative is a story structure based on the audience's mentality and beyond the audience's psychological expectations. At the level of narrative combination, it can often reflect strong regularity. The narratives of American dramas, especially the popular American dramas in recent years, are intentionally or unintentionally breaking the narrative regularity that has been accepted by the audience. That is to break the psychological expectations of the audience. After watching movies for many years, the audience has developed expectations and subtle recognition of a certain film rhythm. Using the theoretical explanation in communication, a clear audience cultivation has been produced., The acculturated audience already has a clear understanding of the direction of the film, the way the lens is expressed, and the structure of the film, and sometimes they are even able to actively mobilize their emotions in order to match the rhythm of the TV series. In recent years, American dramas have been constantly trying to break through the conventional film and television narrative structure on a scientific basis, not only adding plot jumps on the basis of traditional narratives, but also doing a lot of work in breaking traditional narratives. There is transcendence in narrative structure, and there is also transcendence in script. For example, "Breaking Bad" is a typical transcendent structure in terms of subject matter and narrative direction, but the continuous broadcast of "The Big Bang Theory" has a strong contrast in lines and transcendence of audience expectations. It is also very simple, it is the interpretation of one thinking system to another thinking system. Shelton's knowledge and understanding of the problem are all within a fixed cognitive system, so it sounds like that, but if you think about it carefully, there seems to be something wrong.. For example, there is a big V on Weibo called "Director Liu of the Department of Neurology" who left a message under a non-mainstream selfie to reflect such an interpretation. Eyes, looks cool. Director Liu of the Department of Neurology left a message under this photo: If the right eye is not needed, please donate it to those in need. This is the interpretation of one language system to another language system, and if such an interpretation is coherent, it will form the dislocation of language and the transcendence of combination rhythm. Therefore, no matter in terms of the rhythm of film and television editing, the transcendence of narrative logic, or the transcendence of internal language, American dramas have achieved good results in cross-cultural communication, and the source of this effect must be a certain rhythm based on visual forms. beyond.

② Intense sensory stimulation brought by extreme image forms. The extreme image forms referred to here refer to the extremes at the level of design image forms such as the use of scenes and the use of light and shadow, and are a unified description of single extremes and structural extremes. For example, the use of techniques such as close-ups, large panoramas, high-altitude shooting, and jump editing are all part of the extreme image form. What can image extremes bring in cross-cultural communication, or why American dramas always like to choose extreme image forms of expression. What is involved here is the law generally accepted by the audience. Oculodynamics points out that when human eyes receive smooth and regular visual stimuli, the brain will produce a regular signal that weakens comprehension. That is to say, once the visual stimuli form a pattern, the brain will simplify the movement according to this rule, and cannot form a high-level signal. Excitement. For example, psychotherapy such as hypnosis mainly uses this behavior to reduce eye movement stimulation and brain activation. But when the film is received and watched, this kind of large-scale stimulation is needed, and this stimulation mainly comes from the change of scene and so on. If people are regarded as creatures with cultural attributes, then brain science is a typical pure biological research that ignores cultural attributes, so it is easier to find out the universal commonality of human acceptance in such research, then cross-cultural acceptance That's where it comes from. Therefore, in the production process of American dramas, it is understandable to use such visual forms more often. In the American drama "Game of Thrones", the visual spectacle that often appears is the grand narrative, which often jumps from one person to a super-large scene for grand narrative. The macro scene shot at high altitude already has a shocking effect, plus the previous one The extreme editing of the shots highlights the magnificence of this spectacle. For example, in the American dramas "Prison Break" and "Blind Spot", the main character is covered with tattoos all over his body. A physical spectacle is created to stimulate the audience's senses. During the entire production process, American dramas create a visual experience of great contrast through spectacle creation, grand narrative, and great contrast. In the American drama "House of Cards", the male protagonist often looks at the camera, creating an effect that is basically not used in previous film and television works, which achieves the most direct interaction with the audience, although this kind of interaction that breaks through the frame is It is a bit risky, but the effect achieved is also in line with the reality of the whole TV series. This is a TV series with pan-political themes, so in the whole visual communication process, it is the most critical one to directly point to people's hearts and hold them close. When the protagonist casts his gaze and sight outside the picture frame, it breaks the psychological presupposition of the audience, and second, it brings an unprecedented visual experience and interactive participation through this bold breakthrough. It can be said that, The information that can be conveyed by the momentary communication and interaction between the actors and the audience is completely reflected by the innovation of this visual form. Therefore, under the premise of the common biological nature of human beings, the extreme visual impact and visual experience can greatly put aside cultural differences, and directly achieve the maximum cohesion of the audience in the content and screen of film and television dramas. In the field, and form a common sense of resonance, when watching a TV series, cultural differences are considered as unimportant factors. Only in the visual form can it be better played and achieved. It can also be said that the extremeization of visual forms is an important way to cause differences in cross-cultural communication.

③ Awaken thinking and emotional resonance of human beings from different cultures

American dramas not only formed an attempt to break the combination rhythm and visual experience in terms of visual form, but also reflected the deep cultural acculturation effect in cross-cultural communication. While we have seen visual enjoyment through American dramas, we are also gradually accepting the value system, discourse system and life concepts conveyed through American dramas. Through the political context, we can easily draw the analysis of cultural invasion, cultural hegemony and even cultural imperialism pointed out by the Frankfurt School. This is a critical perspective from the perspective of absolute equality, but in today's globalization, Our country is also encouraging the establishment of a community with a shared future for mankind. We need to examine the world and the circle of cultural integration we are in with a diverse and inclusive perspective, and work together to build a cultural community. Taking this as a premise, we must first look at the cultural characteristics brought by American dramas. American dramas and Hollywood movies are both strong American thinking genes. In the process of dissemination, science, usage, and Western democracy are the main cultural characteristics. The superiority of the sense of technology drives the superiority of the way of thinking, and the recognition of its culture is driven by the superiority of the way of thinking and life experience. This idea has always been the main idea of the United States in foreign cultural dissemination or cultural export. In this process, people of different cultural attributes have deepened their sense of identity with American culture through American dramas. Coupled with the grand discourse system that cannot be verified and is occasionally falsified, it has created an important advantage in the spread of American culture. What role did American dramas play in this process? It can be said that film and television works are an important part of this cultural advantage, which is mainly reflected in two aspects. One is the awakening of thinking, and the other is emotional resonance. sense of identity.

First of all, think about awakening, three examples, one is "House of Cards", the second is "The Big Bang Theory" and the third is "Desperate Housewives", which embodies political thinking and life thinking. This is a pragmatic perspective of life, a profound life operation of a grand narrative, "The Big Bang Theory" conveys the coexistence of multiple ways of thinking, the embodiment of the conflict and coexistence of one way of thinking and another way of thinking, "Desperate Housewives" is a reflection on the awakening of modern women's rights and life. In fact, when almost all modern American TV dramas and films are broadcast, they provide solutions to life and ways of thinking. In the films, they are expressed as sharp language and conflicts in stories. The problems to be solved are how to look at big things and how to deal with small things. Things, how to deal with the relationship between people and the world, makes people think, and what awakens the audience is a kind of introspection of life. From this perspective, it can be said that American dramas are a mirror, a mirror that can reflect life, and teach the audience how to think about life. Face your life. Although the methods conveyed in American dramas are not necessarily correct, they are systematic, complete, and have clear American national concepts. The result of continuous dissemination is that their core cultural values will be considered and repeated by the audience. Thinking about it will deepen the recognition. American dramas can have a domesticating effect on the audience, allowing the audience to think about American culture and American values.

Second, emotional resonance. In the process of cross-cultural communication, the emotional resonance caused by vision is the basis for acceptance. Humans are emotional animals, and human needs for emotions are the most unexplainable scientifically, such as love, including love between opposite sexes, family love, friendship love, etc., such as anger, such as patriotism, and so on. Some people say that most American film and television works have the main theme. Although this statement is a bit extreme, it is not unreasonable. From Hollywood to American dramas, most of the thoughts running through it are indeed the main theme led by American culture. Culture may not be widely recognized, but the lack of emotion transcends cultural attributes. Human beings are emotional animals. As long as they are human, they have emotional needs, needs to love and be loved, etc. So what American dramas have been trying to do is to create this kind of emotional resonance and emotional stimulation. To create emotional resonance is to create agreement, and artistic expression in visual form is the best way to create emotional resonance beyond cultural attributes. There is a Chinese poem: the lonely smoke in the desert is straight, this feeling of boundlessness, expressed in five words, is right Personally speaking, the images produced are extremely rich, and Chinese people know that this is good, but for people with other cultural attributes, it may be difficult to understand, and they will find it difficult to evoke even a big desert. What kind of aesthetic imagery? For example, the aesthetic imagery conveyed by the four words "Mountain Dance Silver Snake" is a very rich description of natural landscapes. It can be said that we have used the beauty of words to the extreme, but the beauty of the picture must be expressed through the form. It shows that American dramas are experts in using visual forms to convey aesthetics and create visual images. Almost all American dramas with better communication effects have this simple form of expression to achieve an aesthetic picture that arouses the audience's thinking. But it is worth noting that the emotional resonance conveyed by the visual form of American dramas does not pursue absolute unity and resonance, but its pursuit is open. That is to say, in the entire image creation process, the pursuit of aesthetics is greater than the pursuit of specific aesthetics. Pursuing a holistic image trend without forcing a clear aesthetic image is also a very important feature of American dramas in the dissemination of visual forms. Through the expression of visual forms, the grand aspect can reach the grand emotional resonance with the producer, and the micro level can achieve the same emotional resonance as empathy in terms of emotional shaping, allowing the audience to eliminate cultural differences, educational differences and even wealth differences to achieve complete communication, followed by the systematic dissemination of the way of thinking under the premise of emotional resonance, and American values such as science, democracy, and pragmatism. It can also be said that American drama is a seeding machine in cross-cultural communication, and it is also a seeding machine that works tirelessly and repeatedly. It passes American culture through the path of emotional resonance, thinking system identification, and cultural identity, and repeatedly affects the audience. Cultivation makes the audience reject other cultures in the process of thinking about what to do and whether it is right or wrong. Thinking about one thing is more important than accepting one thing. Only thinking about one thing means complete acceptance. Criticism is also a kind of accept embodiment.

Therefore, in the process of cross-cultural communication, American dramas use visual forms of expression and the creation of visual spectacle to obtain the psychological resonance of the audience and consolidate the values to be disseminated. On this basis, we need to reflect and learn a lot. The first is tolerance. Look at the problem objectively, don't have colored glasses to reject a certain culture, but choose to understand, accept and research, followed by learning, learning the advantages of American TV dramas in visual form, and using them as soon as possible, and being able to experience and understand them in the process of using them. Create visual forms of art with its own cultural attributes. After all, as long as it is an image you can see, there is room for innovation and creation. The tide of globalization is becoming more and more turbulent. In this process, we must accept and learn the advantages of other civilizations with an inclusive attitude, so as to better build an image community.

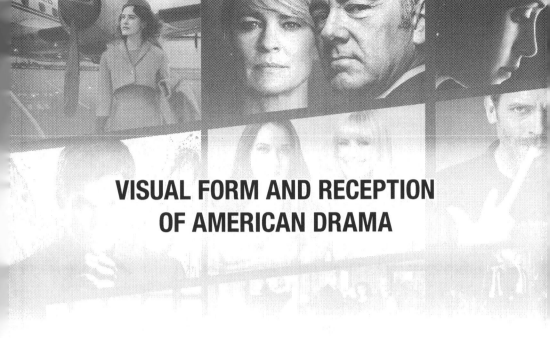

VISUAL FORM AND RECEPTION OF AMERICAN DRAMA

VISUAL FORM FEATURES AND INNOVATIONS OF AMERICAN TV DRAMAS

1. The characteristics and aesthetics of visual art

The visual form of American TV series and the visual form of the image we have studied. In this article, we focus on the art form of TV series. To grasp the connotation of the art form of TV series, we must first start with the form. The so-called form refers to the equal function of the physical form and the psychological form, that is, the internal form can express the function of the external form. In other words, it expresses the relationship between the external form and the internal form, and becomes a form. [1]We regard form as the self-expression of inner emotion, combined with the original state of external form, the combination of the two forms the connotation of form. Form has two meanings, one is natural form, which is equated with the "shape" of a thing. One is an abstract form, which refers to a certain structure, relationship, or whole formed by interdependent factors, and refers to a certain arrangement that forms a whole, that is, a logical form.[2]

---

[1] Qian Jiayu. Visual Psychology—Thinking and Communication of Visual Forms [M]. Shanghai: Xuelin Publishing House, 2006, 1, p.7.

[2] Pan Kewu. On the Visual Form of TV Drama[J]. Modern Communication—Journal of Communication University of China, 2009(2).

Simply put, the natural form is equivalent to the original form of things, and the abstract form is inevitably re-synthesized and re-created. Natural form focuses on issues such as composition, symmetry, balance, contrast, perspective, repetition, and color expression at the level of visual aesthetics, and solves the problem of recording and expressing TV drama images in a certain form. This aspect has a very mature concept in film and television creation and techniques.[3]

The creation of aesthetic feeling in visual art is firstly manifested in its external visual form. On this point, Western formalism aesthetics has quite a lot of discussion. For example, Clive Bell, a famous art critic in the early 20th century, clearly stated in his book "Art" that beauty is a "significant form". The form composition method in visual communication design is the most basic type of modal language in visual communication design, so what is the specific form of expression of this modal language structure? Generally speaking, the composition of formal beauty is mainly expressed in visual communication design It consists of the following two parts, one is the perceptual material that constitutes the beauty of form, and the other is the law of combination between the perceptual materials that constitute the beauty of form. The perceptual materials that constitute the beauty of form in visual communication design are mainly the colors, lines, shapes, etc. in the picture. These elements are the basis of visual communication design works, and they themselves have a certain sense of formal beauty. For example, color is a constituent element with strong formal beauty. [4]Regarding the significance of color as an indispensable constituent element to aesthetic art, this article will be involved in the following chapters.

For visual art, the visual form includes two levels from the inherent nature and structural relationship, namely the surface visual form and the deep visual form. The surface visual form is the element of the material medium of artworks, including line, color, texture, light and shadow, shape and space, etc. These aspects are exactly what Heidegger called the "material factors" that exist in all artworks. The deep visual form

[3] Pan Kewu. On the Visual Form of TV Drama[J]. Modern Communication—Journal of Communication University of China, 2009(2).
[4] Yu Minyi. Analysis of Modal Structure in Contemporary Visual Communication Design [J]. Sichuan Drama, 2018(04).

is the internal level of visual art, that is, the relationship, structure and organization arrangement among the various elements in the space. It mainly studies the relationship and force in the space. Deep visual form is the focus of visual form research, and it is more complex, and finally condensed into the formal beauty rules or visual formal grammar in art and aesthetics, such as proportion, balance, rhythm and so on. [5]Just like Cao Hui's definition of the connotation of visual form: visual form refers to the physical form of sensory objects, such as shape, line, color, space, etc. [6]Entering a new stage of development, at the end of the 19th century and the beginning of the 20th century, this visual form completed the evolution from static to dynamic, such as the current visual art form of TV dramas, which has become an important part of life. The development of intuitive forms caused by visual forms, that is, the development of abstract art and impression art, all prove that forms also have invisible functions. That is to say, through the processing of the ideology of the human brain, the internal psychological form is transformed into the external three-dimensional form and displayed. "The so-called formal expression, there are three ways of expression: figurative expression; abstract expression; more abstract expression. If the image and form of the image belong to the form of image expression, it is impossible to have an instant visual change. If the image image If the form is abstract, then it must be the form of instantaneous visual changes." [7]In combination with Professor Qian Jiayu's statement, the composition of TV dramas is the two forms of "watching" and "imagining" that constitute the visual form of TV dramas. TV series is an art form mainly based on visual effects. Creators organize life elements, add their own understanding, endow connotations higher than life, and use visual art means to touch the hearts of the audience, so as to arouse the audience's enthusiasm. Recognize and empathize, and obtain the aesthetic value of visual art.

---

[5] Liu Wen. Visual Form of TV Drama: From Object to Path[J]. China Television, 2018(01):51-56.

[6] Cao Hui. Aesthetic Research on Visual Forms——A Survey of Visual Forms Based on Western Visual Art [M]. Beijing: People's Publishing House, 2009, 3.

[7] Pan Kewu. On the Art Form of TV Dramas. Modern Communication—Journal of Communication University of China[J], 2009, 4.15.

ANALYSIS OF THE VISUAL CHARACTERISTICS
OF AMERICAN DRAMAS

The main manifestations of American dramas in terms of visual form are: 1. Appropriate rhythm: appropriate rhythm of the picture and psychological rhythm; 2. Contrast of movement in the picture: aesthetics of movement in the picture;

1. Appropriate rhythm: the rhythm of the picture and the psychological rhythm are appropriate

Catherine George wrote in one of his books: "Rhythm is to us what the ghost of Hamlet is to the guards at night, often incomprehensible and elusive. When we seek it, He doesn't show up, and when we're talking about other things, he's there—but fleetingly. The rhythm is charismatic in its very nature, but like a ghost, it doesn't come on call. [8]" From the side, it shows that rhythm is a dominant form just like the melody of music. At the same time, we give rhythm to the living body—generally speaking, rhythm is everywhere in our life, ranging from the cycle of seasons to the structure of human life characteristics. Every breath of the human body, every beat of the pulse, and every relaxation of the blood vessels are the powerful rhythm of life. Rhythm exists not only in the trivial daily life of the human body, but also in the spiritual and cultural life of the human body. When discussing rhythm as aesthetics, many scholars also attribute rhythm to aesthetics. For example, Yan Qianhai once confirmed this point of view in his book. According to his view, in a series of aesthetic or philosophical categories of Lao Tzu, Tao and image, existence and non-existence, emptiness and reality, taste and wonder, metaphysics and nature, these opposing concepts have been unified in Tao, which is the embodiment of a rhythm concept. [9]And his statement comes from "Lao Tzu": "Everyone in the world knows that beauty is beautiful, but it is

---

[8] Yan Qianhai. The Art Form of TV Dramas [M]. Shanghai: Fudan University Press (Professional Series of Broadcasting and TV Directing), 2009.1.
[9] Yan Qianhai. Film and Television Literary Criticism [M]. Guangzhou: Huacheng Publishing House, 2016.2.

evil; everyone knows that good is good, but this is not good. Therefore, existence and non-existence are born together, difficulty and easy are complementary, long and short are the same, high and low are the same. Ying, the sound and sound harmonize, follow each other."

The rhythm in film and television culture also has its expressive power. As far as TV dramas are concerned, "The rhythm of TV dramas is based on the dramatic conflicts in the works and the emotional state of the characters, using various expressive techniques of TV art to form dynamic and static, dynamic and dynamic, static and static in montage sentences or montage paragraphs., fast and slow, long and short, strong and weak, etc., to produce an orderly "pulse" beat, and through the audience's physiological perception and then affect the audience's aesthetic emotion. In a TV series, rhythm is not Dispensable, it plays the role of 'breathing' and 'heartbeat' in the work." The rhythm [10]of TV dramas includes narrative structure (plot rhythm, action rhythm, character change rhythm), picture rhythm and sound rhythm. Generally speaking, the narrative rhythm determines the picture rhythm and sound rhythm, and the picture rhythm and sound rhythm affect the rhythm of certain paragraphs. The formation of picture rhythm is inseparable from camera movement, picture composition, and montage theory, while the formation of sound rhythm is inseparable from sound, sound effects, music and other elements. Sound is also controlling the rhythm of TV dramas. The basic characteristics of the rhythm of the voice include the pitch of the voice, where music can be added, the length of dialogue lines, and the speed of speech, etc. The main goal pursued by TV dramas is to combine the rhythm of moving pictures with the rhythm of sound through the rhythm of montage, so as to achieve the organic unity of vision and hearing. From this point of view, sound effects may not be the main purpose of TV dramas, but they have undeniable The role of neglect. There is another kind of rhythm, Yan Qianhai called it "reverse sound-picture rhythm" in "The Art Form of TV Dramas" (the film and television industry has always had the theory of sound-picture counterpoint. The so-called opposition refers to the opposite of the picture in terms of rhythm and speed. Music, forming the complex rhythm and speed between visual image and auditory image. But after all, the opposition is

---

[10] Wang Weiguo. Aestheticization of Thought [M]. Beijing Broadcasting Institute Press, 2004.

5

borrowed from musical terms, which always reminds people of music and is quite incomprehensible to ordinary people. More importantly, sound and picture Counterpoint is not aimed at rhythm), [11] that is, the rhythm of the three parts of sound, picture, and editing produces different degrees of difference. The use of "reverse sound and picture rhythm" has deepened the visual and auditory image of TV dramas. American dramas break through the traditional structure and composition, break the audience's conventional psychological rhythm in terms of rhythm and rhythm, and pursue a brand-new psychological contrast in order to achieve the effect of attracting audiences. For example, in the American drama "House of Cards", irregular shooting and editing methods are often chosen. There are four aspects to grasp the rhythm of visual form

First, visual rhythm. This visual rhythm is inseparable from basic elements such as light, composition, and color. The visual rhythm of TV is further divided into the rhythm of light in vision and the rhythm of movement in vision. Light makes us see this colorful world, makes us feel all the warmth and cold, makes us experience the ups and downs of life, and at the same time, creates the lens and picture of TV. Grasp the visual light and darkness, color and gray, depth and light, and you have already grasped part of the rhythm of the TV series.

Second, the plot rhythm. "Plot, the word according to the current popular meaning, is the comprehensive arrangement of events in the story or things that have happened." Aristotle was the first to combine the rhythm of the plot with philosophical aesthetics so as to The person who expressed the relationship between the three. [12] Therefore, the plot rhythm of the TV series not only affects the final direction of the plot but also grasps the psychology of the audience. If movies are a condensed summary of art, then TV dramas are a detailed description of life. From this simple definition, it requires that the plot rhythm of TV dramas pay more attention to details than the plot rhythm of movies, so that they can be more delicate. The performance of life-like elements. As the audience, what they value in the plot of the movie is the overall macro plot rhythm.

---

[11] Yan Qianhai. The Art Form of TV Dramas [M]. Shanghai: Fudan University Press (Professional Series of Broadcasting and TV Directing), 2009.1.

[12] Yan Qianhai. The Art Form of TV Dramas [M]. Shanghai: Fudan University Press (Professional Series of Broadcasting and TV Directing), 2009.1.

On the contrary, they pay more attention to the "small plot" in the content of TV dramas. Movies can delete those secondary or dispensable plots, but TV dramas are different. It is those secondary plots in TV dramas that enrich the overall plot of TV dramas, thus constituting the main body of TV dramas.

Third, emotional rhythm. However, the emotional rhythm of TV dramas can be divided into three categories: one is the emotional expression of the characters in the play; the other is the emotional expression of the creative subject; Control the level that the public's aesthetic emotions can reach in a specific time period and in a specific situation, so as to obtain the unanimous approval of the aesthetic object. The first is the visual rhythm of the TV series. This visual rhythm is inseparable from basic elements such as light, composition, and color. The visual rhythm of TV is further divided into the rhythm of light in vision and the rhythm of movement in vision. Light makes us see this colorful world, makes us feel all the warmth and cold, makes us experience the ups and downs of life, and at the same time, creates the lens and picture of TV. Grasp the visual light and darkness, color and gray, depth and light, and you have already grasped part of the rhythm of the TV series. The second is the plot rhythm of the TV series. "Plot, the word according to the current popular meaning, is the comprehensive arrangement of events in the story or things that have happened." Aristotle was the first to combine the rhythm of the plot with philosophical aesthetics so as to The person who expressed the relationship between the three. [13]Therefore, the plot rhythm of the TV series not only affects the final direction of the plot but also grasps the psychology of the audience. If movies are a condensed summary of art, then TV dramas are a detailed description of life. From this simple definition, it requires that the plot rhythm of TV dramas pay more attention to details than the plot rhythm of movies, so that they can be more delicate. The performance of life-like elements. As the audience, what they value in the plot of the movie is the overall macro plot rhythm. On the contrary, they pay more attention to the "small plot" in the content of TV dramas. Movies can delete those secondary or dispensable plots, but TV dramas are different. It is those secondary plots in TV dramas that enrich the overall plot of TV dramas,

---

[13] Yan Qianhai. The Art Form of TV Dramas [M]. Shanghai: Fudan University Press (Professional Series of Broadcasting and TV Directing), 2009.1.

thus constituting the main body of TV dramas. Another is the emotional rhythm of the TV series. However, the emotional rhythm of TV dramas can be divided into three categories: one is the emotional expression of the characters in the play; the other is the emotional expression of the creative subject; Control the level that the public's aesthetic emotions can reach in a specific time period and in a specific situation, so as to obtain the unanimous approval of the aesthetic object.

Fourth, intellectual rhythm. According to the characteristics of TV, the role of the audience is the "passive" side, making movie watching a single passive behavior, but in fact it is not the case. The audience does not accept all the content of the TV. Not only "watching", but also thinking, which requires that TV dramas are no longer a reproduction of life, but that creators need to integrate intellectual elements into the overall creation. Modern psychology divides intelligence into general intelligence and special intelligence, crystalline intelligence and liquid intelligence, content intelligence, product intelligence and operational intelligence, component intelligence, experiential intelligence and situational intelligence, Gardner's eight intelligences (logic, language, Naturalism, Music, Space, Body Movement, Interpersonal, Inner), and Emotional Intelligence, which has become a mantra, etc. [14]Intelligence in TV dramas refers to the fact that the characters in the drama not only have comprehensive intelligence, but also focus on a certain aspect of intelligence, such as intelligence in experience and situations., dialogue and other aspects of intellectual control.

How to control the development of the rhythm? For actors, the speed of the characters' movements, the speed of speech, and the change of emotions; Composition processing; for post-production, the use of synchronous sound, the combination of shots, the addition of sound, etc. are all very important. Of course, in film and television works, this is just a generalization of rhythm on a macro level. Grasping the rhythm of the rhythm can not only better shape the roles of the characters in the play, enrich the emotions of the characters, but also cause dramatic conflicts, promote the development of the plot, and make the film and television works more complete in front of the public. Music plays a role in exaggerating the atmosphere and enhancing emotional expression in TV

---

[14] Yan Qianhai. The Art Form of TV Dramas [M]. Shanghai: Fudan University Press (Professional Series of Broadcasting and TV Directing), 2009.1.

drama works of art, and it is also an important element that constitutes the rhythm of TV dramas. In TV drama works of art, different types of music sound serve the storyline and thoughts and feelings of TV dramas. The overall tone of the storyline determines the choice of music sound, but the music sound also has a negative effect on the development of the plot. [15]Compared with the visual form of art, the role of music in TV art works requires the audience to have a stronger self-understanding ability. The information of visual feedback is intuitive and specific, but the emotion of music is abstract, and the creator can influence it subtly. Certain information is conveyed to the audience, which requires the audience to think and perceive so as to communicate with the creator's thoughts. The influence of music on the rhythm of TV dramas is reflected in two aspects. The first point is that TV drama creators use music sound to convey reality or psychological feelings to adjust the rhythm of the plot. The second point is that TV drama works use music sound to express the psychological changes of characters in the play. To put it simply, we will form a fixed combination of music, pictures and emotions. It is impossible to use a soothing and warm tone as the background music for a tense and exciting martial arts scene. As Hu Zhifeng said: "The proper handling of music and sound can, on the one hand, accurately and layeredly reveal, reveal, and exaggerate the psychological fluctuations and fate changes of the characters in the play; The third is to overcome the limitations brought about by the stereotyped characters and environment in the screen, and supplement the fixed "real" part of the play, so that the inner sentiment and charm of the whole play are beautiful. The melody can reach an 'empty' state, which can greatly expand the artistic imagination of the audience."

The rhythm of a TV drama works is as big as the actors, and the use of music in the later stage, as small as the use of lighting props, all play a role that cannot be ignored in regulating the film and television works. The use of lighting occupies a very strong position in the art of TV dramas. The natural light effect shows a natural and more real scene; the dramatic light effect creates a fantasy and exciting atmosphere; when the two kinds of light When used together, there is a rich artistic world full of expressive flavor. The light of most film and television works is artificially

---

[15] Hu Zhifeng. Outline of TV Aesthetics [M]. Beijing Broadcasting Institute Press, 2003.

processed or superimposed and recreated, but we cannot absolutely say that all artificially processed lights are dramatic light effects. This is the charm of light. How to deal with the effect of light depends on how our plot is going. In addition to the use of light, color can also affect people's subjective emotions. For example, red can remind people of blood and sacrifice, and at the same time, it can make people feel enthusiasm and warmth. Black can make people feel quiet, scary and lonely at the same time. Just like our TV series, it is impossible to directly hit the eyes and let the audience's emotions respond to the plot immediately. What the audience needs is a gradual process, and color plays the role of gradually giving people hints. "Color can be created in the The effect of people and objects in conflicting action, and changing rhythms allows colors to flow from one place to another, creating new and surprising effects when other colors collide or blend." Premise of [16]Color It is light, which is a good illustration of the role of light. And how to grasp the rhythm of light also controls the rhythm of color very well.

2. Picture movement contrast: the aesthetics of picture movement

Rhythm is the rhythm of structure. In a general sense, structure refers to the collocation and arrangement of the various components of things. The structure of a TV series is the way in which TV materials are collocated and arranged. The structure of TV dramas is mainly a collocation and arrangement in the time dimension. The arrangement of materials is a kind of combination of front and back, which is temporal and elapsed. The components of a TV series are diverse, including shots, sound, subtitles, etc. Therefore, it presents a multi-dimensional world.[17]

The structure of TV series is the means and form by which the creators endow the material with meaning and interpretation. A good creator should not only have good creative ideas, but the connotation and meaning he gives to the work is the living soul of a film. At the same time, how to use

---

[16] Color Film and Colored Films, Dreyer in Double Reflection [M], New York: Dutton, 1973

[17] Tian Qi. A Brief Analysis of the Structure of TV Dramas [J]. China Television, 2010(05):82-83.

the charm of lens language to explain the creator's ideas is very important. The quality of a TV series and the depth of ideological significance depend not only on the content of the shooting, but also on the editing and combination of the content. The creativity of the editing team can play the role of icing on the cake, making the original good content more exciting, and some ordinary content can also be played better. On the contrary, if the editing combination lacks practical experience and creativity, it may ruin the original very good material and make the original wonderful content lose its due effect. The emphasis here is on the importance of post-production of TV dramas, but the evaluation of TV dramas is not limited to post-editing. Of course, the structure of a TV drama is determined by the content. The complexity and changeability of life itself, the wide variety of writers and artists' understanding of life, aesthetic pursuit, and artistic taste will inevitably make the structure of TV dramas diverse and colorful. For example, the cross-reminiscence structure of multiple perspectives and multiple characters in the new era, the network structure of multiple clues interweaving, the candied haws-style series structure of connecting people or events, and the psychological structure beyond time and space, etc. wait. The artistic personality of TV dramas, the unique way of thinking and montage means of TV dramas provide the most powerful conditions for the ever-changing structural forms. The most basic and common structures are the following: one is the dramatic structure, also known as the traditional structure. It satisfies the appreciation psychology of people who like to read stories with beginning and end, and builds a balanced bridge between the appreciation subject and the appreciation object; the second is the prose structure, emphasizing the documentary of life and the authenticity of emotion, focusing on lyricism; the third is the psychological structure, this kind of structure has a jumping plot, fast rhythm, and large span, which can save space, expand capacity, show the intricacies of life, and reveal the spiritual journey of characters; ", breaking the limitation of the "fourth wall" in the stage play. It mobilizes the audience's sense of participation, further enhances the sense of reality and documentary, makes the audience feel friendly, and easily arouses association and thinking, fully embodying the unique advantages of TV dramas.[18]

---

[18] Yao Li.Multiple Forms of TV Drama Structure in the New Era-Series of TV Drama Studies[J].Film Literature,1996(05):60-62.

"Morphological structure" mostly refers to the external organization method of the play, that is, the method of combining many stories of future TV dramas, which is the last complete step to make the play take shape, including how to deal with the division and connection between stories and stories, events and stories, Sequence and arrangement; stipulate the proportional arrangement of basic structural elements such as beginning, development, climax, and ending; determine the division and combination of scenes, etc. American film and television theorist Robert McKee divided the play structure into several parts in the form of graphs in the book "Story-Material, Structure, Style and the Principles of Screenplay": a series of "actions" constitute "events"; Transform "events" into "scenes"; connect "scenes" with "scenes"; combine them into "acts" according to a certain "beat"; then connect "acts" into "story"; finally combine "story" into " drama".[19]

In a broad sense, people's cognition of things includes both static and dynamic aspects. As far as visual art is concerned, the transition from surface form to deep form is not static, but a dynamic process, and the medium and intermediate link that promotes its transformation is "force". We call this force motion. As the way things exist, movement is also a means of transitioning from the surface to the depth and simulating the real three-dimensional space in two-dimensional space. When we add the concept of sports to film and television works, it is not difficult to see that the essential meaning of sports still applies to film and television works.

As a dynamic visual art, TV drama not only has its unique personality, but also has the commonality of most visual art works. Works of visual art are based on objective things, coupled with subjective ideas. How to interpret the connotation of visual art works well, we cannot deny that this process is inseparable from the subjective consciousness of the audience, which includes personal social experience and aesthetic taste. But the most critical thing is the subjective idea of the creator, that is, something that the creator wants to convey to the audience. The visual form of graphic art is mainly expressed in pictures and paintings. Berenson notes: "Painting is an art that gives a lasting impression of artistic truth in only two dimensions. The painter, therefore, must consciously do what we all

---

[19] Gao Jinsheng. Analysis on the Structure Types of Long-form TV Series[J]. China Television, 2004(01).

do unconsciously - construct his three-dimensionality. Also As Riegl once emphasized in "The Problem of Style": "All artistic activities begin with the impulse to imitate and directly reproduce the real appearance of natural things. Ancient humans wanted to present things as three-dimensional for the purpose of Make sure of it. "Compared with graphic art, video movement has added the dimension of time, which is an expansion of a visual form in multiple dimensions of time.[20]

Dynamic visual art is a sublimation of static visual art. As Cao Hui said, "It is a combination of time and space. Every freeze frame of a dynamic picture is a static visual art work. In other words, Every movement of a static picture is a dynamic visual art work. [21]Every dynamic film and television picture is completed by the combination of many moving or static different objects. The formation of simple visual power is not enough to fundamentally control the film and television picture The visual form expression in dynamic images should be based on visual principles, through the coordination and comparison of visual power among the various elements in the image, and create corresponding visual forms according to the different needs of plot expression. There are various ways of formal expression in dynamic images, but the common point of these formal expressions is that in the process of formal expression, visual principles are combined to arrange the dynamic visual power accordingly. Although the production of visual power has certain physical Attributes, but it is mainly determined by people's psychological reactions. The grasp of visual power in dynamic images must be based on different film and television creation themes and different plot expression needs to create a perfect visual form in the film and television screen in a reasonable distribution.[22]

In the creation of TV dramas, video movement adds the dimension of time, which is an expansion of visual forms in multiple dimensions of time. Video movement includes camera movement, actor movement,

---

[20] The Application of Visual Art and Aesthetic Concepts in TV Dramas [J], Contemporary Television, 2002(01).

[21] Cao Hui. Aesthetic Research on Visual Forms——A Study on Visual Forms Based on Western Visual Art[M]. Beijing: People's Publishing House, 2009,3.

[22] Wang Nannan.Visual form expression in moving images[J].Film Literature,2008(19):31-32.

comprehensive movement of actors and cameras, and editing to form a dynamic composition. First of all, the movement of the camera can record the state of the subject, and there is a real form in expressing the speed, time and space of the subject. Secondly, through the movement of the camera, the original static or dynamic things are represented, and the picture has a richer three-dimensional sense from multiple directions. Finally, the movement of the camera can also express the psychological state of the subject and endow it with expressiveness. To sum up, as Mr. Wang Weiguo said in his book "Into the TV Series - Wang Weiguo's Selected Works": "Camera movement narrative is to narrate and express emotions through the form of movement." Secondly, actor movement [23]is After the actors receive the script, based on their understanding of the characters in the script, coupled with the director's requirements for the presentation of film and television works, the expression of the content of the script based on the feedback of the actor's subjective ideology. Then, the comprehensive movement of the actors and the camera is a process in which the camera and the actors cooperate with each other to capture each other. The cameraman and actors need to cooperate to fulfill the director's requirements, and complete their own tasks inside and outside the camera. Finally, there is editing movement, which is the process of reprocessing and recreating the formed dynamic composition. It is the creation of film and television works that rearrange and synthesize the dynamic image performances completed by actors in front of the camera to express the director's subjective consciousness and objective reality.

There are also many forms of expression in visual art. In the history of painting, realism and abstraction are the two main streams. After the invention of film, various genres of visual art such as realism, surrealism, and aestheticism coexisted and interpenetrated. However, TV art is dominated by the form of realism from the subject matter to the technique, which is determined by the characteristics of TV itself. TV dramas are not news documentaries, and cannot copy and copy life materials. TV artists use the external image of things to express the inner meaning of things through appropriate methods, so as to reproduce the reality of life

---

[23] Wang Weiguo. Into TV Dramas—Wang Weiguo's Selected Works. China Film Publishing House, 2012, July.

instead of the material of life. [24]The art of TV dramas is the use of image movement to transform static graphic art into a dynamic visual art form. Film and television works are completed in the form of dynamic vision. Although the principle of plane vision can simply explain the composition of each moment of the image in the form analysis, if the dynamic image is placed in a certain period of time for visual expression research, The original plane vision principle is no longer applicable. The visual power of dynamic images can be formed through the comparison of the moving speed, moving rhythm, moving direction, etc. of objects. The grasp of visual power in dynamic images depends on different themes of film and television creation, and the expression of different plots needs to create a perfect visual form in the film and television screen in a reasonable distribution.

3. Accumulated montage: three-dimensional interaction inside and outside the frame

Montage was originally a term derived from architecture, and gradually extended to film and television culture and lens language. According to Professor Li Yulin, the word montage has a broad sense and a narrow sense. The narrow sense refers to the lens combination skills of film and television works. In the broad sense, montage is not only the combination skills mentioned in the narrow sense, but also the unique image of film and television. It refers to the expression of film and television images by writers; secondly, it is a method of layout of film and television works for narrative methods, space-time structures, etc.; then, it refers to the combination and combination relationship between pictures and sounds; finally, It is also the composition of the picture represented by the combination of shots. Therefore, we say that montage is an artistic technique for film and television to reflect reality and a unique thinking language for film and television.

As we know Eisenstein's montage theory: In Eisenstein's view, the meaning of montage is not only attributed to the selection and rhythmic

---

[24] The Application of Visual Art and Aesthetic Concepts in TV Dramas [J]. Contemporary Television, 2002(01).

organization and association, nor is it only attributed to the connection of plot elements. Eisenstein's montage theory holds that the juxtaposition of the two shots and their inner conflict will produce a third factor—an opportunity for ideological evaluation of the depicted things. That is, the new chemical reaction produced by the combination of separate montage paragraphs, the magical chemical reaction between paragraphs acts on the expressive function of things. Eisenstein summed up the function of montage as: "a logical and coherent narrative" that "can be as exciting as possible". [25]Susan Lange said: "Once the rhythm is confirmed, it is implemented in the entire space of the film. It is born from the artist's original concept of 'allegory' and runs through the main part of the work... The whole act is a kind of The form of accumulation..." For the processing of rhythm, it can be completed in one montage paragraph, or in multiple montage paragraphs. Of course, each montage paragraph can be regarded as an independent individual, each individual montage paragraph bears its own rhythm, and each montage paragraph has its own narrative task, which is processed and processed to form a complete plot with mutual relations, with full rhythm. Even though each individual montage has its own emotional tone, it does not deviate from the theme. At the same time, we must also pay attention to the fact that combining the rhythms of several montage passages requires an accurate grasp of the inner emotional rhythms of the characters in the play. The emotional tone of the characters is based on the overall style, so that the montage can play a role.

Montage is inseparable from the use of long shots. Long shots are an artistic expression that comprehensively uses the photographic means of "push, pull, shake, move, follow, rise, and fall" to record the whole process of scene scheduling. Long shot theory is also called "paragraph shot theory" which refers to a long, continuous shooting of a scene or a scene, so as to truly and completely express the thoughts of the objective world. The famous scholar Bazin has his own set of theories about long shots. He believes that the nature of movies is the restoration of the objective world. Dramatic omissions based on causality should be abandoned, and reality should be reproduced in a complete and natural way without cutting things off. time and space of occurrence. After World War II, French film critic André Bazin raised objections to the role of montage, arguing

---

[25] Eisenstein. On Montage [M]. Beijing: China Film Press, 1998.12.

that montage imposes the director's point of view on the audience, limits the ambiguity of the film, and advocates the use of depth-of-field shots and scene scheduling The continuous shooting of the long-shot film is considered to maintain the integrity of the plot space and the real time flow. Bazin believes that the time-space continuity expressed by long shots is an important means to ensure the realism of movies. Montage's method of decomposition and combination not only destroys the integrity and unity of the object world, simplifies and belittles the reality it depicts, but also draws the audience's attention to the things the director pays attention to. The objectivity of things is replaced by the director's subjectivity, and the complexity of meaning is replaced by unity. The audience cannot be in a position of free choice and independent judgment, the initiative of thinking and evaluation cannot be brought into play, and the room for imagination is lost. Therefore, he believes that reality is ambiguous, and only the use of long shots can provide the audience with the opportunity and right to freely choose the picture. Montage decomposes the complete time, space and events, which is extremely unreal. The director decomposes through montage, adding his own subjective consciousness, and does not allow the audience to choose, so he advocates canceling montage.

Speaking of Bazin's theory of montage and long shot, we have to mention Krakauer's theory: Krakauer extended Bazin's theory. Krakauer established a rigorous theoretical system in the book "The Nature of Film". His central theme is "the restoration of material reality", because he regards film as an extension of photography, and its full function is Document and reveal the world around us, not tell fictional stories. The purpose of his film research is to find out a development route that is most in line with the nature of film through the study of various films. To this end, he analyzed the materials and methods of films in detail, rejected all "non-film" forms and contents, and established his "film" standards. His conclusion is that only by taking a camera to discover and record those typical accidental events in real life can a film in line with the nature of the film be made. Krakauer is considered an important representative of Western realistic film theory, but he The rejection of traditional feature films has caused much controversy. In order to achieve the purpose of "restoration", he only allows films to play the two functions of "recording" and "revealing", and rejects all films designed by artists, with clear ideological intentions, and with a beginning and an end in the story structure. Even experimental films in purely audiovisual form are excluded because, in his opinion, such films tend to avoid telling stories, but they do so with little regard for the closeness of cinematic means, ignoring the intimacy of the camera. they have abolished the principles of the story in order to establish the principles of art, and in this "revolution" perhaps the art gains and the cinema nothing.

Some people call the long shot "montage inside the shot". It can be seen that montage and long shot are completely different creative concepts of separation and combination. Montage uses the division of time and space to achieve the purpose of storytelling, while long shot pursues It is the relative unity of time and space without any artificial explanation; the narrative nature of montage determines the director's self-expression in film art, and the long-shot record determines the director's self-elimination; montage theory emphasizes artificial skills outside the screen, while The long shot emphasizes the inherent original power of the picture; the montage shows the single meaning of things, which is distinctive and mandatory, while the long shot shows the multiple meanings of things, which is instantaneous and random; montage guides the audience to make choices, The long shot prompts the viewer to make a choice. For a long time, the art of montage has always been controversial. Many scholars believe that montage art puts the audience in a passive position, but the most essential difference between the long-shot theory and the montage theory is that the long-shot theory focuses on the audience's psychological real thoughts, allowing the audience to "freely choose their own views on things and events." explain". Looking at this issue from the standpoint of the audience, it is not difficult for us to see that the characteristics of long shots are to emphasize the ontological attributes and recording functions of movies, to emphasize the authenticity of life, and to belittle the role of formal elements such as plot structure and montage. Although the theory of long shots is highly respected, we cannot just obliterate the contribution of montage theory to film art. Just like Einstein's attitude towards the art of montage: "...the era when montage almost usurped the complete sovereignty in the realm of film expression is long gone. But many people are chasing prey and shouting to 'bury' montage This is also incorrect." (Eisenstein is referring here to the fact that while certain directors and theorists in the 1930s were concentrating on issues such as plot, character structure on screen, and performance creation in film, they With an arguing attitude, he denied some of the artistic principles of the silent film masters in the 1920s, especially the montage as the main means of expression of the film director's art. - Eisenstein) Although Bazin's long-shot theory has a strong impact on the emphasis on film and television works Authenticity has positive meaning, but completely canceling montage is too extreme. The practice of film and TV creation proves that both montage and long shot are needed, and should complement each other and develop together.

After understanding the use of montage and the theories of the two famous scholars, let's analyze the long-shot narrative. In the long-shot narrative, the creator often appears as an observer, keeping calm and objective, and strives to hide the creator's subjective tendency, including his pursuit of aesthetics and his desire for modeling, in the facts recorded objectively. Behind the images, an indirect form of expression is used to make the creation closer to the original appearance of real life, and to avoid the usual concentration and integration of materials in narrative montage. The long shot shows that the creator expresses his own understanding of the shot narrative under the synthesis of self-aesthetics, self-judgment, and self-pursuit. There are no high-level generalizations, no clips showing a neatly structured plot.

Secondly, the long-shot narrative content is rich and comprehensive. The long-shot narrative attaches great importance to the organic connection between the characters and the daily life environment. Many plots unfold in real life in the streets and alleys. There are many environmental shots, and there are often more procedural shots. What we can observe is that the use of long shots by creators in movies or TV dramas is mostly a long-term macroscopic performance of the environment, or shooting the state of the subject, or explaining the intention of the subject procedural long shot. Not only can it be truly reproduced, but at the same time, the audience can fully receive the creator's infection after seeing it through this narrative mode.

Then, the long shot is close to the perspective of ordinary people, adopts natural light effects, and pays attention to the recording of simultaneous sound, and strives to reproduce real life and real characters by maintaining the unity and continuation of time and space. Those modeling treatments that can make the audience aware of a certain artistic effect should be carefully avoided, and strive to be true and natural. What can move people the most is often the most real thing. Whether the long shot takes advantage of it or its uniqueness, it can bring the audience into the artistic effect it wants to express for a long time.

The narrative of the long shot, then, is a narrative that focuses on photography. Long shots use photography to complete the narrative, usually in the process of changing the shooting angle and adjusting the distance of the scene, using one lens to complete the tasks of a group of lenses in the montage narrative. Therefore, many expressions of ideas are conceived and realized in continuous photography. This requires the creator to use the feature of long-shot narrative after understanding the intention he wants to express, and to cooperate with the narrative of the shot to achieve a different filming without changing the angle and distance of other filming factors. Intermittent full narrative mode.

In the end, we all know that the narrative of long shots is an optional and open narrative. What the long lens records is an original ecology close to real life, and adopts a plain and simple photography technique, which gives the audience a sense of closeness and participation in life, so the audience may make their own creations based on the images provided on the screen. Evaluation and Conclusions.

In fact, generally speaking, the narrative of the long shot and the narrative of montage have the same parts, but also have different parts. Just like the narrative of the long shot we mentioned above, montage also has its narrative method: the narrative of montage has creative The subjectivity of the author is to edit and recombine all my screen shots to what I want it to express; it is not as rich as a long shot, on the contrary, montage is a streamlined expression; and montage is artificially reproduced Formal expression, it does not have the requirements of long-shot and demanding reality, as long as it can express the creator's intention; if long-shot is a narrative that focuses on photography, then the biggest difference between montage is that it is a narrative that focuses on editing : Each shot is an independent part of it, there is no connection, and the process of establishing connection after editing. This is the different narrative expression of montage and long shot. We can see that montage pays attention to editing, combination and reproduction, while long shot focuses on reality and nature. But they also have the same identity. Whether we use montage or long shots, we aim to give the audience a sense of immersion that is close to reality when watching. We cannot say that montages are unreal, because long shots are also Through the expression after the design and mise-en-scène, the design itself is a kind of montage, so the two are consistent in themselves. We cannot deliberately emphasize long shots and ignore montage for the sake of reality, or demand montage for exaggerated and strong artistic expression without paying attention to the use of long shots. Effective use of the differences and identities between them will collide with different feelings.

VISUAL FEATURES IN THE CREATION PROCESS OF AMERICAN DRAMA

At present, with the continuous development of media technology, the influence of global media on social life is becoming more and more extensive. Human culture has gone through a process from ancient to modern times, from language to text, and Gutenberg's invention of metal movable type printing brought writing to the center of culture [26]. Today, each of us is surrounded by electronic screens. Whether it is going to work, commuting, or leisure, we can't escape the electronic screens. The flow of pixels is intertwined with complex information. Scholars in informatics, sociology, literature, communication and other disciplines are more or less studying how to use this inch-square screen to transmit information better, faster and more efficiently. Similarly, in Hollywood, the world's best film and television drama workers are working day and night on how to better use visual forms to tell stories, shape characters, create environments, and render atmospheres.

Freud believes that the formation of dreams will go through four stages, including "compression", "displacement", "imagery", and "retouching". And these four processes seem to coincide with the workflow of film and television drama workers to a certain extent.

---

[26] Kelly. Inevitable [M]. Beijing: China Industry and Information Technology Publishing Group, 2016. pp: 91.

1. Compression

The so-called "compression" means that a variety of hidden ideas are compressed into an expressible picture form, and the process of compression is to achieve the direct transmission of visual content. This seems to be like the work of screenwriters. They reprocess the original literary stories and occasional social phenomena with the help of their own art, and turn them into scripts suitable for film and television creation. In Freud's idea, the compression process of dreams is mainly obtained from the extraction of subconscious dream-making materials. It should be noted that the compression does not mean that the obvious dream is just a simple simplification and refinement of the hidden dream, but a transformation and transformation of the original dream material, which can almost be said to be a completely different version.

Take the American drama "The Band of Brothers" (The Band of Brothers) as an example, which is adapted from the novel of the same name. Although the original work is a memoir based on Ambrose's interviews, veterans' family books and historical materials, the producers Tom Hanks and Steven Spielberg still respect the original work and make a comprehensive review of the original work. Made a drastic adaptation. This is because compared to the volume of the original work, the capacity of the ten-episode TV series is relatively limited, and the carrying capacity of the picture is incomparable to the text. Although the events that appear in the TV series can be found in the original work, not everything can be represented in the TV series.

Take the action "Recruit Support" in the fourth episode of the show as an example.

The fourth episode is mainly about the Allied forces' "Market Garden" operation, which corresponds to the eighth chapter "Hell's Highway" in the original book. In the original book, the author introduces in detail the primary goal of the 506th Regiment where Company E belongs and the tasks of the airborne troops in the "Market Garden" operation, and even introduces the importance and danger of the entire battle. Combined with some other relevant historical materials, readers can easily deduce the key nodes of the "Market Garden" operation and the specific reasons for its final failure. Through the TV series, these contents are briefly mentioned in the film, and it is difficult for the audience to see the reason for the failure of the plan. The goal of the entire campaign was only succinctly elaborated and summarized by Winster "The entire European vanguard has stopped to allocate resources for this operation. This is Montgomery's personal plan." This way of creation is like soldiers in war. They can only see the specific tasks they are performing in front of them. The deployment and consideration of the entire campaign or even the strategy seems to them to be almost non-existent concepts.

In the pre-battle mission briefing, the director uttered a line "I don't think they will cancel this battle" through the mouth of the character Nick. If you just look at this line, it is difficult for the audience to understand what this line means. But in the original book, in fact, in that summer, the Allied forces canceled more than a dozen combat operations of the airborne division, and all of them were temporarily canceled when the combat troops were about to board the plane, because the ground troops had already entered the destination. In fact, the audience needs to combine this line with what Winster said above that the entire European vanguard has stopped, so that it is possible to understand what Nick's sentence means. But this kind of passing line is really easy to be ignored, and it is difficult for the audience to capture the specific thoughts of the producer. In contrast to the original text, the author gave a detailed description of the phrase "cancellation of operations", explaining the preparation and cancellation of each combat operation. That is to say, the concept detailed in the original text was canceled in the TV series. The author can't help but suspect here that the producers may be trying to use this specious and semantically unclear expression to express the confusion of each soldier who performs specific tasks in the war, just like the audience's confusion when watching TV dramas.

On the contrary, in the original book, for Randleman who was shot in the shoulder and did not evacuate in time, the TV series used a certain amount of space to describe how he spent the night hiding in the barn with difficulty, and also A Dutch couple was constructed to help and take care of him properly, and even jointly killed a German soldier who was exploring the barn. These contents do not appear in the original text, and all the content in the original text is just a short paragraph "Randelman in the forward position was shot in the shoulder and fell behind. He hid in a barn, a German soldier Running in after him, Randleman stabbed him with a bayonet, killed him, covered the body in hay, and then he covered himself in hay."

This technique is used again by the writers in the sixth episode "Bastogne".

The sixth episode "Bastogne" corresponds to the eleventh chapter of the original book "They Surrounded Us——These damn bastards". The original book described the experience of the entire E company in the Ardennes Forest like a group, and objectively described what each soldier saw and heard in that difficult winter. In the episode, almost the entire episode focuses on the hygienist Eugene. Through Eugene's perspective, the producer showed the damage caused by the war to everyone. It is almost difficult for the audience to remember the names of everyone who was injured or even killed, but they all appeared in front of Eugene alive. In this episode, the producers even arranged a seemingly "romantic" encounter for Eugene: due to Eugene's duties, he often had to go back and forth between the front line and the field hospital, so Eugene met a female nurse. But then the field hospital was destroyed by a nighttime bombardment, and Eugene only found the girl's iconic blue headscarf in the ruins, and such a token that could commemorate the dead also disappeared in this episode——Eugene Because of the enemy's siege, the gauze was already in short supply. After a little hesitation, he used the turban as gauze to bandage his comrades. At this moment, Eugene's dedication to work, and even the bravery and fearlessness of every soldier in the war, were fully demonstrated by the producers.

The author believes that the source of this episode must correspond to the only text describing Eugene in the original text: "He is there wherever he is needed, and you often don't know how he got there. His bravery, his dedication to the wounded Heroic rescue has never been recognized.... I only know that if any soldier deserves a medal for fighting in the cold, fighting in the ice and snow, and shuttling in the wilderness and forest under the fire of bullets, it must be our medic. gold"

The above two examples correspond to Freud's point of view: "compression is the deformation and transformation on the original basis". When screenwriters write scripts, they will have an original fantasy opportunity. These opportunities are usually unconscious ideas or certain plots and experiences, and then compress the scattered ideas into a point, and then start from this point to dig out suitable themes, story frames, styles, forms, etc. The author believes that the fourth episode "Recruit Support" corresponds to "Chaos", and "Bastogne" corresponds to "Cruel". As Thomas Harrison, the screenwriter of Hannibal, said, when he creates a script, he will first generate an intention or inner motivation, and then deconstruct the connotation of the theme according to this intention or inner motivation, and then give the characters and inner motivation according to the theme. The plot, and then there is the overall framework. The so-called story is the connecting line of the whole plot, which connects these fragmented consciousnesses to form a whole, and at the same time makes the actions and details of the characters more specific, which is conducive to the expression of the picture.

2. Two, displacement

The so-called "displacement" is to express the dream material in the subconscious through deformation, makeup, etc. This method can be summarized as metaphor, symbol and other rhetorical techniques in literary and artistic creation. The preconscious surveillance system creeps into the realm of consciousness. Playwrights often express this kind of metaphor through the design of some props, so as to complete the transmission of cultural or background information. But relatively, when watching this kind of interpretation, viewers need to have a certain cultural or knowledge background in order to better interpret the hidden content that the playwrights want to express.

From this point of view, displacement seems to be transforming some important content into irrelevant content, or abstracting abstract concepts or concrete objects into a symbolic symbol. From the perspective of psychoanalysts, in the process of displacement of manifest dreams, they often cover up something important in the unconscious and replace it with insignificant content., to dig out the deep connotation and psychological activities in hidden dreams.

From the perspective of film and television drama personnel, the process of displacement and the behavior of psychoanalysts are exactly reversed in order. In order to cater to the censorship of the censors, or to maintain a certain kind of "political correctness", the playwrights often have to hide their inner wishes, thoughts or emotions in the film and television dramas, and the displacement just gives them a an outlet for self-expression. Specifically, using montage or props in the play as a medium, the playwrights can implicitly express their true thoughts through the plot.

Take the famous American drama "The Wire" (The Wire) as an example. In this American drama with a total of five seasons, the director and director focus on describing a class of American society or social reality in each season. For example, the first season focused on describing the life in the slums, and the screenwriter used fried chicken food as an important prop to express the character's connotation and even culture. In the play, a newcomer goes to a banquet in a high-end restaurant. Because he cannot adapt to the cumbersome etiquette in the high-end restaurant, he feels that his self-esteem has been frustrated. After the banquet, he insists on eating a fast food to regain his self-esteem. In terms of character background, although the newcomer has relatively superior family conditions in the black group, because his parents are drug dealers, although the family income is acceptable, he still cannot really integrate into the upper class. Plus, a low-level drug cartel figure assumes that if fried chicken is so popular, whoever invented it must be rich. In his leader's view, people who fry chicken are just like people who make drugs. They can't become real rich people. Only by mastering the chain of drug sales can they become real bosses. And this point of view has also been confirmed in another American drama "The Breaking Bad" (The Breaking Bad). Under the guise, he became the biggest drug lord in this drama. It seems that the screenwriter wants to use fried chicken to prove that although Flynn seems to be an executive of a chain fried chicken restaurant, in fact, his drug trafficking behavior and the label of fried chicken mean that he is still a wandering at the bottom of society. people. At the same time, it also seems to express a meaning that among the lower-class people in the United States, the popularity of drugs can almost be compared with that of fried chicken.

Here, the screenwriters of this play directly convey the American street culture and the preferences of the people at the bottom of society to the audience through the visual element of "fried chicken". This design quickly brings the audience closer to the characters in the play The psychological distance also allows the audience to better understand the character and motivation of the characters. But it should be noted that, as mentioned above, this kind of visual expression requires the viewer to have a certain amount of cultural or knowledge accumulation, so this also causes some works to be sought after in the academic or professional fields, but often the market feedback is not good. one of the reasons.

In the classic American drama "The Sopranos" (The Sopranos), which has won 14 Emmy Awards and 4 Golden Globe Awards, the playwrights used the story of the underworld boss Tony to actually describe the ubiquitous male middle-aged crisis: mother and child Discord, husband and wife fights, work crisis. In the first episode of the show, Tony saw a group of ducks flying into the swimming pool at home while having breakfast, so he rushed into the pool to play with the ducks happily, and one day later, when he experienced After a change of job, a grumpy mother, a wayward child, ignoring his wife and the priest who seemed to be "tangled" with his wife, in the afternoon when everything seemed calm, when he saw the ducks in the pond again, he was shocked. Suddenly fainted. The author believes that the duck here seems to imply the purest emotion in Tony's heart, which is his simple sustenance in the face of nature and the world as a simple man. But when he faced the "innocence" in his heart again after experiencing the boredom and pain of society, he could only faint because he could no longer return to that innocence. In the end, he had no choice but to bite the bullet and go on, otherwise he could only faint and die, giving up everything.

At the same time, there is a colloquial phrase "So what?" (What do you gonna do?) that appears frequently in this play. When Tony learned that a healthy person died suddenly while sitting on the toilet; when Tony confided to his psychiatrist that his child suddenly chose to commit suicide, but failed because the rope was too long; While the phone is on fire, when you have to arrange robbery, car theft, and murder tasks for your subordinates, at this moment, in addition to bravely facing the various disadvantages brought by life, you can only comfort yourself with "what can I do?"

It can be said that any audience who has watched this gangster movie, after experiencing the family problems, natural disasters and man-made disasters described in the play, it seems that it is not so difficult to think about the underworld things the protagonist does. accept. It seems that everyone has their own helpless choices when doing anything, and the motivation for anything cannot be attributed to a simple reason. The mafia is just one of the many professions in American society. Everything that Tony experienced in the play may even be experienced by the audience in their lives. The author guesses that this may be one of the reasons why this work was so popular in the United States. one.

3. Imaging

The so-called visualization of dreams is to turn thoughts into images, and TV dramas also need to go through the process of transferring thoughts to words and then converting them into images. The quality of the picture finally presented in the two-dimensional picture frame directly determines the quality of the work of the entire crew.

Similarly, in the fourth episode of "Band of Brothers", in order to show the welcome of the Dutch for the arrival of the Allied forces, the director added a plot in addition to the commonly used welcome scenes in the lane when making the film: when the soldiers of Company E When searching houses at night, a family of civilians was found hiding in the basement of their house, and a soldier gave the child a piece of chocolate. When the child took the chocolate torn open by his father and smiled with satisfaction after eating it, the director used a close-up close-up of the face with a long shot of nearly 10 seconds to show the change in the child's expression. The camera well portrays the welcoming attitude of the Dutch civilians towards the Allied forces. It is enough for the audience to remember the innocent smile of the child.

In addition, when the Dutch people welcomed the Allied forces, the director arranged a scene where the Dutch people punished the women who had shown favor to the German soldiers. When a woman was stripped of her coat and her hair was forcibly shaved off The director adopted a subjective shot of a soldier of Company E who was mixed in the crowd. He looked beyond the human wall formed by the onlookers and saw the crying face of the woman, the hands plucking her hair, and the surrounding Crowd's angry facial expressions.

These two sets of shots seem to tell the audience the cruelty of war.

Whether it is a child who lived to be four years old before eating chocolate for the first time, or a weak woman with a good figure, no one can escape the influence of war, and no one can escape. the hardships of war.

In addition, when the soldiers of Company E marched along the road on the second day, the picture first focused on the wild flowers on the side of the road, and then the camera slowly panned up. The foreground of the shot remains with wildflowers along the road.

At this moment, both the soldiers present and the audience seemed to have an "illusion" that the war was going well and all suffering was about to end. The author believes that this kind of calm and peaceful emotion is what the director wants to convey to the audience through the screen. And when the enemy suddenly appeared and Company E was defeated and had to retreat in embarrassment, the director used four consecutive close-up shots to express the emotions of the soldiers of Company E: the first shot was a close-up shot of a hand wiping blood on their pants as It started, then moved up, aiming at the expression of a soldier who had just seen his comrade die beside him. He was still staring blankly at the distant battlefield, as if he hadn't recovered from the fright. Afterwards, the screen pans to the left, a soldier has empty eyes, clasped his hands, and seems to be praying silently; the second shot is a fixed shot, a soldier's face is covered with blood, bowing his head silently, and another comrade-in-arms is frowning, concerned He punched the former's shoulder with his fist as if first, and then slowly hugged the former; the third shot started with a close-up of a soldier's face. He first looked at the battlefield just now, and then silently closed his eyes and bowed his head. The mouth seemed to be cursing, and then the camera panned to another soldier. The soldier in the picture opened his mouth slightly, his eyes were dull, and he seemed completely unaware of what happened just now; the fourth shot first focused on a soldier The soldier wept silently, and then the camera panned up, and the camera was aimed at another soldier. His face was full of reluctance and expectation, as if he still hoped that the missing comrade would appear in his eyes. The continuous use of these images, combined with the slow pace, all show the emotions of all soldiers facing a failed battle. It can be said that focusing on expressing the feelings of each individual in the battlefield is the theme that the entire production team wants to express. They will not be stereotyped in recreating famous battles in history, but just want the audience to feel that they are independent people in the war. What are the nuanced feelings.

At the same time, compared to dreams, TV dramas can not only stimulate human vision, but auditory stimulation is also a very important factor to consider. In addition to having excellent pictures, it is also very important to match auditory elements that are suitable for a good film and television drama a link. This is because in real life, in addition to vision, hearing is also an important way for us to experience the world. The cooperation of vision and hearing often makes the world in the plot more "plausible".

Take the first season of the American TV series "Stranger Things" (Stranger Things) as an example. When a few friends at the end of the third episode know that their good friend Will has passed away, the soundtrack - David Bowie's "Heroes" - crescendo, "We can be heroes, just for one day", as a classic song in the 1970s, in addition to being used as a footnote for this play (the story of this play is set in the 1980s s), as David Bowie's famous song dedicated to Berlin, especially the Berlin Wall, there is a kind of courage against the world. And here, although the pictures are exaggerating the sadness of the friends, the use of this song seems to suggest to the viewers: Will may not have died, he has been fighting hard in the dark, against with terror. Similarly, at the beginning of the fourth episode, although the sadness at the end of the previous episode still continues, everyone believes that Will is no longer in this world, except for one person-Will's mother. With a mother's intuition and various signs, she still believes that Will is alive and needs her to find him and save him. At this time, the soundtrack of the opening title sounded "Atmosphere" by Joy Division. It means to face the darkness and fragility of the heart and fight against it. Combined with the development of the plot later, and looking back at the use of these two songs by the crew, we have to applaud the crew's ingenious arrangement.

In the first episode of "The Sopranos", in the plot where Tony fainted in his backyard, the picture first showed Tony having a barbecue in his backyard, preparing to spend a wonderful afternoon, and after playing in the swimming pool at home, he flew The walking ducks cross-edited, and at this time the music suddenly joined an aria from the first act of the Italian opera "Swallows" composed by Puccini. Combining with the

31

smiling Tony in the picture, he gradually felt dizzy, and the ducks in the pond flew away one by one. The feeling of powerlessness that yearns for life but cannot be grasped. Especially when Tony gradually felt dizzy and was about to fall, with the soprano singing "Mio Sogno, mia vita" (this is Italian: my dream, my life), followed by the The music was cut to a halt as the barbecue grill exploded due to overturned fuel.

This ingenious arrangement, if it is not for a certain understanding of Italian opera, the audience may just think that the use of Italian opera here is simply rendering Tony as the background of the Italian mafia. And when the viewer understands the general idea of the opera used here and the content of the lyrics, the whole drama's portrayal of a man's sense of powerlessness in the face of a mid-life crisis is presented in a small segment of the first episode. vividly displayed in front of the viewer.

Based on this, the author believes that American TV drama producers' grasp of images and their consideration of picture and sound are no less than the production level of a movie. There is no element that has nothing to do with the theme, and all the techniques are related to the theme. Matching, each American drama has its unique world view, and the display of these world views is achieved by the production staff's grasp of the visual elements.

4. Retouching

Freud believes that dream embellishment is to filter out the part of the unconscious that is difficult to move through the censorship of the preconscious defense system, otherwise it will disturb the tranquility of the dream, thereby waking the audience from the dream. Another function of embellishment is to arrange and process unconscious materials in a relatively orderly manner, making dreams more smooth and full of logic. And this is just like the post-editing and special effects processing in the creation of American dramas.

In terms of editing, American dramas have gradually continued the standard of the film industry. The editing points and the movement inside and outside the screen lens cooperate with each other, making the rhythm of the whole film natural and smooth, making the audience more immersed in the "dream" and not feeling the false existence.

Still taking Band of Brothers as an example, there are a total of 27 clips in the battle scene from the 27th to the 28th minute of the fourth episode, and only 12 clips in the nighttime house search from the 23rd to the 24th minute point. The above is just a simple example, which is used to illustrate the cooperation between the editing point and the plot, to cover up the bluntness of the jump between shots, and to make the narrative of the screen clearer and more coherent.

In terms of post-production special effects processing, take the American drama "House of Card" (House of Card) as an example. In this drama, in order to express certain emotions or create a certain atmosphere, the composition is very particular. For example, in order to show the majesty of state power, a large number of centered and symmetrical compositions are used.

The above are just a few brief examples of the 73-episode American drama in 6 seasons. In fact, these seemingly exquisite compositions are almost all the credit of the later stage. According to relevant information, House of Cards has used RED EPIC and Dragon series digital cameras as its main shooting machines since the first season. This machine can shoot 5K (5120*2700) resolution images. That is to say, when shooting on the set, the photographer does not have to consider the absolute symmetry of the composition at all. As long as the arranged scenes are shot according to the needs, the post-producers will cut out an absolutely symmetrical picture based on the 5K material. That's it, because the ultra-high material resolution provides sufficient redundant space for the trimming of the later screen.

Also, in order to show the darkness of the political world, from the first season, the producers have worked together to create a dark feeling for the whole film, but this does not mean that the color is not transparent. At the same time, although the color of this film is not very strong, it is still obvious enough. Whether it is the wine red tie or the background color of sea foam, it contains a lot of wisdom and labor of the colorist.

VISUAL ART AND SOUL OF
AMERICAN DRAMA

THE VISUAL IMAGERY OF AMERICAN DRAMAS——
THE RHYTHMIC RESONANCE OF VISION AND SOUL

The visual form of American TV series and the visual form of the image
we have studied. In this article, we focus on the art form of TV series.
To grasp the connotation of the art form of TV series, we must first start
with the form. The so-called form refers to the equal function of the
physical form and the psychological form, that is, the internal form can
express the function of the external form. In other words, it expresses
the relationship between the external form and the internal form, and
becomes a form. [27]We regard form as the self-expression of inner emotion,
combined with the original state of external form, the combination of the
two forms the connotation of form. Form has two meanings, one is natural
form, which is equated with the "shape" of a thing. One is an abstract
form, which refers to a certain structure, relationship, or whole formed by
interdependent factors, and refers to a certain arrangement that forms a
whole, that is, a logical form. [28]

Simply put, the natural form is equivalent to the original form of
things, and the abstract form is inevitably re-synthesized and re-created.

---

[27] Qian Jiayu. Visual Psychology—Thinking and Communication of Visual Forms
[M]. Shanghai: Xuelin Publishing House, 2006, 1, p.7.
[28] Pan Kewu. On the Visual Form of TV Drama[J]. Modern Communication—
Journal of Communication University of China, 2009(2).

Natural form focuses on issues such as composition, symmetry, balance, contrast, perspective, repetition, and color expression at the level of visual aesthetics, and solves the problem of recording and expressing TV drama images in a certain form. This aspect has a very mature concept in film and television creation and techniques.[29]

The creation of aesthetic feeling in visual art is firstly manifested in its external visual form. On this point, Western formalism aesthetics has quite a lot of discussion. For example, Clive Bell, a famous art critic in the early 20th century, clearly stated in his book "Art" that beauty is a "significant form". The form composition method in visual communication design is the most basic type of modal language in visual communication design, so what is the specific form of expression of this modal language structure? Generally speaking, the composition of formal beauty is mainly expressed in visual communication design It consists of the following two parts, one is the perceptual material that constitutes the beauty of form, and the other is the law of combination between the perceptual materials that constitute the beauty of form. The perceptual materials that constitute the beauty of form in visual communication design are mainly the colors, lines, shapes, etc. in the picture. These elements are the basis of visual communication design works, and they themselves have a certain sense of formal beauty. For example, color is a constituent element with strong formal beauty. [30]Regarding the significance of color as an indispensable constituent element to aesthetic art, this article will be involved in the following chapters.

For visual art, the visual form includes two levels from the inherent nature and structural relationship, namely the surface visual form and the deep visual form. The surface visual form is the element of the material medium of artworks, including line, color, texture, light and shadow, shape and space, etc. These aspects are exactly what Heidegger called the "material factors" that exist in all artworks. The deep visual form is the internal level of visual art, that is, the relationship, structure and organization arrangement among the various elements in the space. It mainly studies the relationship and force in the space. Deep visual

[29] Pan Kewu. On the Visual Form of TV Drama[J]. Modern Communication—Journal of Communication University of China, 2009(2).
[30] Yu Minyi. Analysis of Modal Structure in Contemporary Visual Communication Design [J]. Sichuan Drama, 2018(04).

form is the focus of visual form research, and it is more complex, and finally condensed into the formal beauty rules or visual formal grammar in art and aesthetics, such as proportion, balance, rhythm and so on. [31]Just like Cao Hui's definition of the connotation of visual form: visual form refers to the physical form of sensory objects, such as shape, line, color, space, etc. [32]Entering a new stage of development, at the end of the 19th century and the beginning of the 20th century, this visual form completed the evolution from static to dynamic, such as the current visual art form of TV dramas, which has become an important part of life. The development of intuitive forms caused by visual forms, that is, the development of abstract art and impression art, all prove that forms also have invisible functions. That is to say, through the processing of the ideology of the human brain, the internal psychological form is transformed into the external three-dimensional form and displayed. "The so-called formal expression, there are three ways of expression: figurative expression; abstract expression; more abstract expression. If the image and form of the image belong to the form of image expression, it is impossible to have an instant visual change. If the image image If the form is abstract, then it must be the form of instantaneous visual changes." [33]In combination with Professor Qian Jiayu's statement, the composition of TV dramas is the two forms of "watching" and "imagining" that constitute the visual form of TV dramas. TV series is an art form mainly based on visual effects. Creators organize life elements, add their own understanding, endow connotations higher than life, and use visual art means to touch the hearts of the audience, so as to arouse the audience's enthusiasm. Recognize and empathize, and obtain the aesthetic value of visual art.

---

[31] Liu Wen. Visual Form of TV Drama: From Object to Path[J]. China Television, 2018(01):51-56.

[32] Cao Hui. Aesthetic Research on Visual Forms——A Survey of Visual Forms Based on Western Visual Art [M]. Beijing: People's Publishing House, 2009, 3.

[33] Pan Kewu. On the Art Form of TV Dramas. Modern Communication—Journal of Communication University of China[J], 2009, 4.15.

(1) The structure of the visual form of American dramas

In a general sense, structure refers to the collocation and arrangement of the various components of a thing. The structure of a TV film is the collocation and arrangement of TV materials. The structure of TV films is mainly a collocation and arrangement in the time dimension. The arrangement of materials is a kind of combination of front and back, which is temporal and elapsed. The components of a TV film are diverse, including shots, sounds, subtitles, etc. Therefore, it presents a multi-dimensional world.[34]

The structure of the TV film is the means and form by which the creators endow the material with meaning and interpretation. A good creator should not only have good creative ideas, but the connotation and meaning he gives to the work is the living soul of a film. At the same time, how to use the charm of lens language to explain the creator's ideas is very important. The quality of a TV film and the depth of ideological significance depend not only on the content of the film, but also on the editing and combination of the content. The creativity of the editing team can play the role of icing on the cake, making the original good content more exciting, and some ordinary content can also be played better. On the contrary, if the editing combination lacks practical experience and creativity, it may ruin the original very good material and make the original wonderful content lose its due effect. The emphasis here is on the importance of post-production of TV shows, but the evaluation of good or bad TV shows is not limited to post-editing. Of course, the structure of a TV show is determined by the content. The complexity and changeability of life itself, the wide variety of writers and artists' understanding of life, aesthetic pursuit, and artistic taste will inevitably make the structure of TV dramas diverse and colorful. For example, the cross-reminiscence structure of multiple perspectives and multiple characters in the new era, the network structure of multiple clues interweaving, the candied haws-style series structure of connecting people or events, and the psychological structure beyond time and space, etc. wait. The artistic personality of TV dramas, the unique way of thinking and montage means of TV dramas provide the most powerful conditions for the ever-changing structural forms. The most basic and common structures are

---

[34] Tian Qi. A Brief Analysis of the Structure of TV Films[J]. China Television, 2010(05):82-83.

the following: one is the dramatic structure, also known as the traditional structure. It satisfies the appreciation psychology of people who like to read stories with beginning and end, and builds a balanced bridge between the appreciation subject and the appreciation object; the second is the prose structure, emphasizing the documentary of life and the authenticity of emotion, focusing on lyricism; the third is the psychological structure, this kind of structure has a jumping plot, fast rhythm, and large span, which can save space, expand capacity, show the intricacies of life, and reveal the spiritual journey of characters; ", breaking the limitation of the "fourth wall" in the stage play. It mobilizes the audience's sense of participation, further enhances the sense of reality and documentary, makes the audience feel friendly, and easily arouses association and thinking, fully embodying the unique advantages of TV dramas.[35]

Knowing the structure of TV, we say that "morphological structure" refers to the external organization of the play, that is, the method of combining many stories in the future TV series. The division and connection, sequence and arrangement of stories; the proportion arrangement of basic structural elements such as beginning, development, climax and ending; determining the division and combination of scenes, etc. American film and television theorist Robert McKee divided the play structure into several parts in the form of graphs in the book "Story-Material, Structure, Style and the Principles of Screenplay": a series of "actions" constitute "events"; Transform "events" into "scenes"; connect "scenes" with "scenes"; combine them into "acts" according to a certain "beat"; then connect "acts" into "story"; finally combine "story" into " drama".[36]

1. Exercise

In a broad sense, people's cognition of things includes both static and dynamic aspects. As far as visual art is concerned, the transition from surface form to deep form is not static, but a dynamic process, and the

---

[35] Yao Li.Multiple Forms of TV Drama Structure in the New Era-Series of TV Drama Studies[J].Film Literature,1996(05):60-62.

[36] Gao Jinsheng. Analysis on the Structure Types of Long-form TV Series[J]. China Television, 2004(01).

medium and intermediate link that promotes its transformation is "force". We call this force motion. As the way things exist, movement is also a means of transitioning from the surface to the depth and simulating the real three-dimensional space in two-dimensional space. When we add the concept of sports to film and television works, it is not difficult to see that the essential meaning of sports still applies to film and television works.

As a dynamic visual art, TV drama not only has its unique personality, but also has the commonality of most visual art works. Works of visual art are based on objective things, coupled with subjective ideas. How to interpret the connotation of visual art works well, we cannot deny that this process is inseparable from the subjective consciousness of the audience, which includes personal social experience and aesthetic taste. But the most critical thing is the subjective idea of the creator, that is, something that the creator wants to convey to the audience. The visual form of graphic art is mainly expressed in pictures and paintings. Berenson notes: "Painting is an art that gives a lasting impression of artistic truth in only two dimensions. The painter, therefore, must consciously do what we all do unconsciously - construct his three-dimensionality. Also As Riegl once emphasized in "The Problem of Style": "All artistic activities begin with the impulse to imitate and directly reproduce the real appearance of natural things. Ancient humans wanted to present things as three-dimensional for the purpose of Make sure of it. "Compared with graphic art, video movement has added the dimension of time, which is an expansion of a visual form in multiple dimensions of time.[37]

Dynamic visual art is a sublimation of static visual art. As Cao Hui said, "It is a combination of time and space. Every freeze frame of a dynamic picture is a static visual art work. In other words, Every movement of a static picture is a dynamic visual art work. [38]Every dynamic film and television picture is completed by the combination of many moving or static different objects. The formation of simple visual power is not enough to fundamentally control the film and television picture The visual form expression in dynamic images should be based on visual principles, through the coordination and comparison of visual power among the various

---

[37] The Application of Visual Art and Aesthetic Concepts in TV Dramas [J], Contemporary Television, 2002(01).

[38] Cao Hui. Aesthetic Research on Visual Forms——A Study on Visual Forms Based on Western Visual Art[M]. Beijing: People's Publishing House, 2009,3.

elements in the image, and create corresponding visual forms according to the different needs of plot expression. There are various ways of formal expression in dynamic images, but the common point of these formal expressions is that in the process of formal expression, visual principles are combined to arrange the dynamic visual power accordingly. Although the production of visual power has certain physical Attributes, but it is mainly determined by people's psychological reactions. The grasp of visual power in dynamic images must be based on different film and television creation themes and different plot expression needs to create a perfect visual form in the film and television screen in a reasonable distribution.[39]

In the creation of TV dramas, video movement adds the dimension of time, which is an expansion of visual forms in multiple dimensions of time. Video movement includes camera movement, actor movement, comprehensive movement of actors and cameras, and editing to form a dynamic composition. First of all, the movement of the camera can record the state of the subject, and there is a real form in expressing the speed, time and space of the subject. Secondly, through the movement of the camera, the original static or dynamic things are represented, and the picture has a richer three-dimensional sense from multiple directions. Finally, the movement of the camera can also express the psychological state of the subject and endow it with expressiveness. To sum up, as Mr. Wang Weiguo said in his book "Into the TV Series - Wang Weiguo's Selected Works": "Camera movement narrative is to narrate and express emotions through the form of movement." Secondly, actor movement [40]is After the actors receive the script, based on their understanding of the characters in the script, coupled with the director's requirements for the presentation of film and television works, the expression of the content of the script based on the feedback of the actor's subjective ideology. Then, the comprehensive movement of the actors and the camera is a process in which the camera and the actors cooperate with each other to capture each other. The cameraman and actors need to cooperate to fulfill the director's requirements, and complete their own tasks inside and outside the camera.

[39] Wang Nannan.Visual form expression in moving images[J].Film Literature,2008(19):31-32.

[40] Wang Weiguo. Into TV Dramas—Wang Weiguo's Selected Works. China Film Publishing House, 2012, July.

Finally, there is editing movement, which is the process of reprocessing and recreating the formed dynamic composition. It is the creation of film and television works that rearrange and synthesize the dynamic image performances completed by actors in front of the camera to express the director's subjective consciousness and objective reality.

There are also many forms of expression in visual art. In the history of painting, realism and abstraction are the two main streams. After the invention of film, various genres of visual art such as realism, surrealism, and aestheticism coexisted and interpenetrated. However, TV art is dominated by the form of realism from the subject matter to the technique, which is determined by the characteristics of TV itself. TV dramas are not news documentaries, and cannot copy and copy life materials. TV artists use the external image of things to express the inner meaning of things through appropriate methods, so as to reproduce the reality of life instead of the material of life. [41] The art of TV dramas is the use of image movement to transform static graphic art into a dynamic visual art form. Film and television works are completed in the form of dynamic vision. Although the principle of plane vision can simply explain the composition of each moment of the image in the form analysis, if the dynamic image is placed in a certain period of time for visual expression research, The original plane vision principle is no longer applicable. The visual power of dynamic images can be formed through the comparison of the moving speed, moving rhythm, moving direction, etc. of objects. The grasp of visual power in dynamic images depends on different themes of film and television creation, and the expression of different plots needs to create a perfect visual form in the film and television screen in a reasonable distribution.

2. Rhythm

Catherine George wrote in one of his books: "Rhythm is to us what the ghost of Hamlet is to the guards at night, often incomprehensible and elusive. When we seek it, He doesn't show up, and when we're talking about other things, he's there—but fleetingly. The rhythm is charismatic in

---

[41] The Application of Visual Art and Aesthetic Concepts in TV Dramas [J]. Contemporary Television, 2002(01).

its very nature, but like a ghost, it doesn't come on call. [42]" From the side, it shows that rhythm is a dominant form just like the melody of music. At the same time, we give rhythm to the living body—generally speaking, rhythm is everywhere in our life, ranging from the cycle of seasons to the structure of human life characteristics. Every breath of the human body, every beat of the pulse, and every relaxation of the blood vessels are the powerful rhythm of life. Rhythm exists not only in the trivial daily life of the human body, but also in the spiritual and cultural life of the human body. When discussing rhythm as aesthetics, many scholars also attribute rhythm to aesthetics. For example, Yan Qianhai once confirmed this point of view in his book. According to his view, in a series of aesthetic or philosophical categories of Lao Tzu, Tao and image, existence and non-existence, emptiness and reality, taste and wonder, metaphysics and nature, these opposing concepts have been unified in Tao, which is the embodiment of a rhythm concept. [43]And his statement comes from "Lao Tzu": "Everyone in the world knows that beauty is beautiful, but it is evil; everyone knows that good is good, but this is not good. Therefore, existence and non-existence are born together, difficulty and easy are complementary, long and short are the same, high and low are the same. Ying, the sound and sound harmonize, follow each other."

The rhythm in film and television culture also has its expressive power. As far as TV dramas are concerned, "The rhythm of TV dramas is based on the dramatic conflicts in the works and the emotional state of the characters, using various expressive techniques of TV art to form dynamic and static, dynamic and dynamic, static and static in montage sentences or montage paragraphs., fast and slow, long and short, strong and weak, etc., to produce an orderly "pulse" beat, and through the audience's physiological perception and then affect the audience's aesthetic emotion. In a TV series, rhythm is not Dispensable, it plays the role of 'breathing' and 'heartbeat' in the work." The rhythm [44]of TV dramas includes narrative structure

[42] Yan Qianhai. The Art Form of TV Dramas [M]. Shanghai: Fudan University Press (Professional Series of Broadcasting and TV Directing), 2009.1.

[43] Yan Qianhai. Film and Television Literary Criticism [M]. Guangzhou: Huacheng Publishing House, 2016.2.

[44] Wang Weiguo. Aestheticization of Thought [M]. Beijing Broadcasting Institute Press, 2004.

(plot rhythm, action rhythm, character change rhythm), picture rhythm and sound rhythm. Generally speaking, the narrative rhythm determines the picture rhythm and sound rhythm, and the picture rhythm and sound rhythm affect the rhythm of certain paragraphs. The formation of picture rhythm is inseparable from camera movement, picture composition, and montage theory, while the formation of sound rhythm is inseparable from sound, sound effects, music and other elements. Sound is also controlling the rhythm of TV dramas. The basic characteristics of the rhythm of the voice include the pitch of the voice, where music can be added, the length of dialogue lines, and the speed of speech, etc. The main goal pursued by TV dramas is to combine the rhythm of moving pictures with the rhythm of sound through the rhythm of montage, so as to achieve the organic unity of vision and hearing. From this point of view, sound effects may not be the main purpose of TV dramas, but they have undeniable The role of neglect. There is another kind of rhythm, Yan Qianhai called it "reverse sound-picture rhythm" in "The Art Form of TV Dramas" (the film and television industry has always had the theory of sound-picture counterpoint. The so-called opposition refers to the opposite of the picture in terms of rhythm and speed. Music, forming the complex rhythm and speed between visual image and auditory image. But after all, the opposition is borrowed from musical terms, which always reminds people of music and is quite incomprehensible to ordinary people. More importantly, sound and picture Counterpoint is not aimed at rhythm), [45]that is, the rhythm of the three parts of sound, picture, and editing produces different degrees of difference. The use of "reverse sound and picture rhythm" has deepened the visual and auditory image of TV dramas.

If the rhythm of TV series is subdivided, it can be divided into the following four aspects:

First, the visual rhythm of the TV series. This visual rhythm is inseparable from basic elements such as light, composition, and color. The visual rhythm of TV is further divided into the rhythm of light in vision and the rhythm of movement in vision. Light makes us see this colorful world, makes us feel all the warmth and cold, makes us experience the ups and downs of life, and at the same time, creates the lens and picture of TV.

---

[45] Yan Qianhai. The Art Form of TV Dramas [M]. Shanghai: Fudan University Press (Professional Series of Broadcasting and TV Directing), 2009.1.

Grasp the visual light and darkness, color and gray, depth and light, and you have already grasped part of the rhythm of the TV series.

Second, the plot rhythm of the TV series. "Plot, the word according to the current popular meaning, is the comprehensive arrangement of events in the story or things that have happened." Aristotle was the first to combine the rhythm of the plot with philosophical aesthetics so as to The person who expressed the relationship between the three. [46]Therefore, the plot rhythm of the TV series not only affects the final direction of the plot but also grasps the psychology of the audience. If movies are a condensed summary of art, then TV dramas are a detailed description of life. From this simple definition, it requires that the plot rhythm of TV dramas pay more attention to details than the plot rhythm of movies, so that they can be more delicate. The performance of life-like elements. As the audience, what they value in the plot of the movie is the overall macro plot rhythm. On the contrary, they pay more attention to the "small plot" in the content of TV dramas. Movies can delete those secondary or dispensable plots, but TV dramas are different. It is those secondary plots in TV dramas that enrich the overall plot of TV dramas, thus constituting the main body of TV dramas.

Third, the emotional rhythm of the TV series. However, the emotional rhythm of TV dramas can be divided into three categories: one is the emotional expression of the characters in the play; the other is the emotional expression of the creative subject; Control the level that the public's aesthetic emotions can reach in a specific time period and in a specific situation, so as to obtain the unanimous approval of the aesthetic object. The first is the visual rhythm of the TV series. This visual rhythm is inseparable from basic elements such as light, composition, and color. The visual rhythm of TV is further divided into the rhythm of light in vision and the rhythm of movement in vision. Light makes us see this colorful world, makes us feel all the warmth and cold, makes us experience the ups and downs of life, and at the same time, creates the lens and picture of TV. Grasp the visual light and darkness, color and gray, depth and light, and you have already grasped part of the rhythm of the TV series. The second is the plot rhythm of the TV series. "Plot, the word according to the current popular meaning,

---

[46] Yan Qianhai. The Art Form of TV Dramas [M]. Shanghai: Fudan University Press (Professional Series of Broadcasting and TV Directing), 2009.1.

is the comprehensive arrangement of events in the story or things that have happened." Aristotle was the first to combine the rhythm of the plot with philosophical aesthetics so as to The person who expressed the relationship between the three. [47]Therefore, the plot rhythm of the TV series not only affects the final direction of the plot but also grasps the psychology of the audience. If movies are a condensed summary of art, then TV dramas are a detailed description of life. From this simple definition, it requires that the plot rhythm of TV dramas pay more attention to details than the plot rhythm of movies, so that they can be more delicate. The performance of life-like elements. As the audience, what they value in the plot of the movie is the overall macro plot rhythm. On the contrary, they pay more attention to the "small plot" in the content of TV dramas. Movies can delete those secondary or dispensable plots, but TV dramas are different. It is those secondary plots in TV dramas that enrich the overall plot of TV dramas, thus constituting the main body of TV dramas. Another is the emotional rhythm of the TV series. However, the emotional rhythm of TV dramas can be divided into three categories: one is the emotional expression of the characters in the play; the other is the emotional expression of the creative subject; Control the level that the public's aesthetic emotions can reach in a specific time period and in a specific situation, so as to obtain the unanimous approval of the aesthetic object.

Fourth, the intellectual rhythm of TV dramas. According to the characteristics of TV, the role of the audience is the "passive" side, making movie watching a single passive behavior, but in fact it is not the case. The audience does not accept all the content of the TV. Not only "watching", but also thinking, which requires that TV dramas are no longer a reproduction of life, but that creators need to integrate intellectual elements into the overall creation. Modern psychology divides intelligence into general intelligence and special intelligence, crystalline intelligence and liquid intelligence, content intelligence, product intelligence and operational intelligence, component intelligence, experiential intelligence and situational intelligence, Gardner's eight intelligences (logic, language, Naturalism, Music, Space, Body Movement, Interpersonal, Inner), and

---

[47] Yan Qianhai. The Art Form of TV Dramas [M]. Shanghai: Fudan University Press (Professional Series of Broadcasting and TV Directing), 2009.1.

Emotional Intelligence, which has become a mantra, etc. [48]Intelligence in TV dramas refers to the fact that the characters in the drama not only have comprehensive intelligence, but also focus on a certain aspect of intelligence, such as intelligence in experience and situations., dialogue and other aspects of intellectual control.

How to control the development of the rhythm? For actors, the speed of the characters' movements, the speed of speech, and the change of emotions; Composition processing; for post-production, the use of synchronous sound, the combination of shots, the addition of sound, etc. are all very important. Of course, in film and television works, this is just a generalization of rhythm on a macro level. Grasping the rhythm of the rhythm can not only better shape the roles of the characters in the play, enrich the emotions of the characters, but also cause dramatic conflicts, promote the development of the plot, and make the film and television works more complete in front of the public. Music plays a role in exaggerating the atmosphere and enhancing emotional expression in TV drama works of art, and it is also an important element that constitutes the rhythm of TV dramas. In TV drama works of art, different types of music sound serve the storyline and thoughts and feelings of TV dramas. The overall tone of the storyline determines the choice of music sound, but the music sound also has a negative effect on the development of the plot. [49]Compared with the visual form of art, the role of music in TV art works requires the audience to have a stronger self-understanding ability. The information of visual feedback is intuitive and specific, but the emotion of music is abstract, and the creator can influence it subtly. Certain information is conveyed to the audience, which requires the audience to think and perceive so as to communicate with the creator's thoughts. The influence of music on the rhythm of TV dramas is reflected in two aspects. The first point is that TV drama creators use music sound to convey reality or psychological feelings to adjust the rhythm of the plot. The second point is that TV drama works use music sound to express the psychological changes of characters in

---

[48] Yan Qianhai. The Art Form of TV Dramas [M]. Shanghai: Fudan University Press (Professional Series of Broadcasting and TV Directing), 2009.1.

[49] Hu Zhifeng. Outline of TV Aesthetics [M]. Beijing Broadcasting Institute Press, 2003.

the play. To put it simply, we will form a fixed combination of music, pictures and emotions. It is impossible to use a soothing and warm tone as the background music for a tense and exciting martial arts scene. As Hu Zhifeng said: "The proper handling of music and sound can, on the one hand, accurately and layeredly reveal, reveal, and exaggerate the psychological fluctuations and fate changes of the characters in the play; The third is to overcome the limitations brought about by the stereotyped characters and environment in the screen, and supplement the fixed "real" part of the play, so that the inner sentiment and charm of the whole play are beautiful. The melody can reach an 'empty' state, which can greatly expand the artistic imagination of the audience."

The rhythm of a TV drama works is as big as the actors, and the use of music in the later stage, as small as the use of lighting props, all play a role that cannot be ignored in regulating the film and television works. The use of lighting occupies a very strong position in the art of TV dramas. The natural light effect shows a natural and more real scene; the dramatic light effect creates a fantasy and exciting atmosphere; when the two kinds of light When used together, there is a rich artistic world full of expressive flavor. The light of most film and television works is artificially processed or superimposed and recreated, but we cannot absolutely say that all artificially processed lights are dramatic light effects. This is the charm of light. How to deal with the effect of light depends on how our plot is going. In addition to the use of light, color can also affect people's subjective emotions. For example, red can remind people of blood and sacrifice, and at the same time, it can make people feel enthusiasm and warmth. Black can make people feel quiet, scary and lonely at the same time. Just like our TV series, it is impossible to directly hit the eyes and let the audience's emotions respond to the plot immediately. What the audience needs is a gradual process, and color plays the role of gradually giving people hints. "Color can be created in the The effect of people and objects in conflicting action, and changing rhythms allows colors to flow from one place to another, creating new and surprising effects when other colors collide or blend." Premise of [50]Color It is light, which is a good

---

[50] Color Film and Colored Films, Dreyer in Double Reflection [M], New York: Dutton, 1973

illustration of the role of light. And how to grasp the rhythm of light also controls the rhythm of color very well.

Montage was originally a term derived from architecture, and gradually extended to film and television culture and lens language. According to Professor Li Yulin, the word montage has a broad sense and a narrow sense. The narrow sense refers to the lens combination skills of film and television works. In the broad sense, montage is not only the combination skills mentioned in the narrow sense, but also the unique image of film and television. It refers to the expression of film and television images by writers; secondly, it is a method of layout of film and television works for narrative methods, space-time structures, etc.; then, it refers to the combination and combination relationship between pictures and sounds; finally, It is also the composition of the picture represented by the combination of shots. Therefore, we say that montage is an artistic technique for film and television to reflect reality and a unique thinking language for film and television.

As we know Eisenstein's montage theory: In Eisenstein's view, the meaning of montage is not only attributed to the selection and rhythmic organization and association, nor is it only attributed to the connection of plot elements. Eisenstein's montage theory holds that the juxtaposition of the two shots and their inner conflict will produce a third factor—an opportunity for ideological evaluation of the depicted things. That is, the new chemical reaction produced by the combination of separate montage paragraphs, the magical chemical reaction between paragraphs acts on the expressive function of things. Eisenstein summed up the function of montage as: "a logical and coherent narrative" that "can be as exciting as possible". [51]Susan Lange said: "Once the rhythm is confirmed, it is implemented in the entire space of the film. It is born from the artist's original concept of 'allegory' and runs through the main part of the work... The whole act is a kind of The form of accumulation..." For the processing of rhythm, it can be completed in one montage paragraph, or in multiple montage paragraphs. Of course, each montage paragraph can be regarded as an independent individual, each individual montage paragraph bears its own rhythm, and each montage paragraph has its own narrative task, which is processed and processed to form a complete plot with mutual relations, with full rhythm. Even though each individual montage has

---

[51] Eisenstein. On Montage [M]. Beijing: China Film Press, 1998.12.

its own emotional tone, it does not deviate from the theme. At the same time, we must also pay attention to the fact that combining the rhythms of several montage passages requires an accurate grasp of the inner emotional rhythms of the characters in the play. The emotional tone of the characters is based on the overall style, so that the montage can play a role.

When it comes to montage, it is natural to mention the long shot. The long shot is an artistic expression method that comprehensively uses the photographic means of "push, pull, shake, move, follow, rise, and fall" to record the whole process of scene scheduling. Long shot theory is also called "paragraph shot theory" which refers to a long, continuous shooting of a scene or a scene, so as to truly and completely express the thoughts of the objective world. The famous scholar Bazin has his own set of theories about long shots. He believes that the nature of movies is the restoration of the objective world. Dramatic omissions based on causality should be abandoned, and reality should be reproduced in a complete and natural way without cutting things off. time and space of occurrence. After World War II, French film critic André Bazin raised objections to the role of montage, arguing that montage imposes the director's point of view on the audience, limits the ambiguity of the film, and advocates the use of depth-of-field shots and scene scheduling The continuous shooting of the long-shot film is considered to maintain the integrity of the plot space and the real time flow. Bazin believes that the time-space continuity expressed by long shots is an important means to ensure the realism of movies. Montage's method of decomposition and combination not only destroys the integrity and unity of the object world, simplifies and belittles the reality it depicts, but also draws the audience's attention to the things the director pays attention to. The objectivity of things is replaced by the director's subjectivity, and the complexity of meaning is replaced by unity. The audience cannot be in a position of free choice and independent judgment, the initiative of thinking and evaluation cannot be brought into play, and the room for imagination is lost. Therefore, he believes that reality is ambiguous, and only the use of long shots can provide the audience with the opportunity and right to freely choose the picture. Montage decomposes the complete time, space and events, which is extremely unreal. The director decomposes through montage, adding his own subjective consciousness, and does not allow the audience to choose, so he advocates canceling montage.

Speaking of Bazin's theory of montage and long shot, we have to mention Krakauer's theory: Krakauer extended Bazin's theory. Krakauer established a rigorous theoretical system in the book "The Nature of Film". His central theme is "the restoration of material reality", because he regards film as an extension of photography, and its full function is Document and reveal the world around us, not tell fictional stories. The purpose of his film research is to find out a development route that is most in line with the nature of film through the study of various films. To this end, he analyzed the materials and methods of films in detail, rejected all "non-film" forms and contents, and established his "film" standards. His conclusion is that only by taking a camera to discover and record those typical accidental events in real life can a film in line with the nature of the film be made. Krakauer is considered an important representative of Western realistic film theory, but he The rejection of traditional feature films has caused much controversy. In order to achieve the purpose of "restoration", he only allows films to play the two functions of "recording" and "revealing", and rejects all films designed by artists, with clear ideological intentions, and with a beginning and an end in the story structure. Even experimental films in purely audiovisual form are excluded because, in his opinion, such films tend to avoid telling stories, but they do so with little regard for the closeness of cinematic means, ignoring the intimacy of the camera. they have abolished the principles of the story in order to establish the principles of art, and in this "revolution" perhaps the art gains and the cinema nothing.

Some people call the long shot "montage inside the shot". It can be seen that montage and long shot are completely different creative concepts of separation and combination. Montage uses the division of time and space to achieve the purpose of storytelling, while long shot pursues It is the relative unity of time and space without any artificial explanation; the narrative nature of montage determines the director's self-expression in film art, and the long-shot record determines the director's self-elimination; montage theory emphasizes artificial skills outside the screen, while The long shot emphasizes the inherent original power of the picture; the montage shows the single meaning of things, which is distinctive and mandatory, while the long shot shows the multiple meanings of things, which is instantaneous and random; montage guides the audience to make choices, The long shot prompts the viewer to make a choice. For a long time, the art of montage has always been controversial. Many scholars believe that montage art puts the audience in a passive position, but the most essential difference between the long-shot theory and the montage theory is that the long-shot theory focuses on the audience's psychological real thoughts, allowing the audience to "freely choose their own views on things and events." explain". Looking at this issue from the standpoint of the audience, it is not difficult for us to see that the characteristics of long shots are to emphasize the ontological attributes and recording functions of movies, to emphasize the authenticity of life, and to belittle the role of formal elements such as plot structure and montage. Although the theory of long shots is highly respected, we cannot just obliterate the contribution of montage theory to film art. Just like Einstein's attitude towards the art of montage: "... the era when montage almost usurped the complete sovereignty in the realm of film expression is long gone. But many people are chasing prey and shouting to 'bury' montage This is also incorrect." (Eisenstein is referring here to the fact that while certain directors and theorists in the 1930s were concentrating on issues such as plot, character structure on screen, and performance creation in film, they With an arguing attitude, he denied some of the artistic principles of the silent film masters in the 1920s, especially the montage as the main means of expression of the film director's art. - Eisenstein) Although Bazin's long-shot theory has a strong impact on the emphasis on film and television works Authenticity has positive meaning, but completely canceling montage is too extreme. The practice of film and TV creation proves that both montage and long shot are needed, and should complement each other and develop together.

After understanding the use of montage and the theories of the two famous scholars, let's analyze the long-shot narrative. In the long-shot narrative, the creator often appears as an observer, keeping calm and objective, and strives to hide the creator's subjective tendency, including his pursuit of aesthetics and his desire for modeling, in the facts recorded objectively. Behind the images, an indirect form of expression is used to make the creation closer to the original appearance of real life, and to avoid the usual concentration and integration of materials in narrative montage. The long shot shows that the creator expresses his own understanding of the shot narrative under the synthesis of self-aesthetics, self-judgment, and self-pursuit. There are no high-level generalizations, no clips showing a neatly structured plot.

Secondly, the long-shot narrative content is rich and comprehensive. The long-shot narrative attaches great importance to the organic connection between the characters and the daily life environment. Many plots unfold in real life in the streets and alleys. There are many environmental shots, and there are often more procedural shots. What we can observe is that the use of long shots by creators in movies or TV dramas is mostly a long-term macroscopic performance of the environment, or shooting the state of the subject, or explaining the intention of the subject procedural long shot. Not only can it be truly reproduced, but at the same time, the audience can fully receive the creator's infection after seeing it through this narrative mode.

Then, the long shot is close to the perspective of ordinary people, adopts natural light effects, and pays attention to the recording of simultaneous sound, and strives to reproduce real life and real characters by maintaining the unity and continuation of time and space. Those modeling treatments that can make the audience aware of a certain artistic effect should be carefully avoided, and strive to be true and natural. What can move people the most is often the most real thing. Whether the long shot takes advantage of it or its uniqueness, it can bring the audience into the artistic effect it wants to express for a long time.

The narrative of the long shot, then, is a narrative that focuses on photography. Long shots use photography to complete the narrative, usually in the process of changing the shooting angle and adjusting the distance of the scene, using one lens to complete the tasks of a group of lenses in the montage narrative. Therefore, many expressions of ideas are conceived and realized in continuous photography. This requires the creator to use the feature of long-shot narrative after understanding the intention he wants to express, and to cooperate with the narrative of the shot to achieve a different filming without changing the angle and distance of other filming factors. Intermittent full narrative mode.

In the end, we all know that the narrative of long shots is an optional and open narrative. What the long lens records is an original ecology close to real life, and adopts a plain and simple photography technique, which gives the audience a sense of closeness and participation in life, so the audience may make their own creations based on the images provided on the screen. Evaluation and Conclusions.

In fact, generally speaking, the narrative of the long shot and the narrative of montage have the same parts, but also have different parts. Just like the narrative of the long shot we mentioned above, montage also has its narrative method: the narrative of montage has creative The subjectivity of the author is to edit and recombine all my screen shots to what I want it to express; it is not as rich as a long shot, on the contrary, montage is a streamlined expression; and montage is artificially reproduced Formal expression, it does not have the requirements of long-shot and demanding reality, as long as it can express the creator's intention; if long-shot is a narrative that focuses on photography, then the biggest difference between montage is that it is a narrative that focuses on editing : Each shot is an independent part of it, there is no connection, and the process of establishing connection after editing. This is the different narrative expression of montage and long shot. We can see that montage pays attention to editing, combination and reproduction, while long shot focuses on reality and nature. But they also have the same identity. Whether we use montage or long shots, we aim to give the audience a sense of immersion that is close to reality when watching. We cannot say that montages are unreal, because long shots are also Through the expression after the design and mise-en-scène, the design itself is a kind of montage, so the two are consistent in themselves. We cannot deliberately emphasize long shots and ignore montage for the sake of reality, or demand montage for exaggerated and strong artistic expression without paying attention to the use of long shots. Effective use of the differences and identities between them will collide with different feelings.

RECEPTION MECHANISM OF
VISUAL FORM OF AMERICAN DRAMA

The arrival of the era of visual culture marks the transformation and formation of a cultural form, and at the same time marks a change in the aesthetic activities of culture and art—traditional education turns to happy imagination brought by visual stimulation, and the aestheticization of daily life. The increasing diversification of visual culture makes culture a shared and art belongs to the public. The widespread dissemination of today's visual culture has made a new turn in the aesthetic world, and people's aesthetic psychology contains a new sensibility and visual novelty. The viewing pleasure of entertainment satisfies people's basic psychological needs at a lower level, and people's value needs will rise along a certain level. Modern social psychology research shows that "the pursuit of visual pleasure has become the basic needs of the modern public deeply influenced by visual culture". According to the aesthetic characteristics of "postmodernism", the aesthetic world will take a new turn: (1) The transformation of aesthetic subject and aesthetic object. With the permeation of commodity concepts, the boundaries between artists and the public are broken, as long as the public with visual perception ability is not limited by artistic accomplishment and cultural level, they can participate in aesthetic activities. (2) Changes in the way of aesthetics. Due to the qualitative change in the way people participate in works of art, there is also a contradiction between the two ways of concentrating and pastime in the aesthetic process of works of art. Concentration is an individual's worship or appreciation of a certain art category, while the way of pastime is often to form a habit first in the sense of touch, and then guide the vision, which is suitable for the public to accept non-worship art.[52]

When the audience appreciates a work of art, the intuition that always participates in understanding activities and forms the basis of reasoning activities immediately becomes artistic perception, which is a direct, inexpressible and rational intuition. Both concrete and abstract, it is a natural light. This is one of the important characteristics of TV drama acceptance.

The visual form of TV dramas is a special system for the audience to perceive the relationship between various elements in TV dramas through vision, and it is the embodiment of abstract thinking in a certain art form in TV dramas. The visual form of TV series not only affects the creation of TV series, but also restricts the audience's acceptance and way of acceptance.

The audience, as the general public, has already formed a set of personal evaluations of the film even when watching the film, but there is an element of desire for the film to be easy to understand after all. As

---

[52] Cheng Wenguang. The Transformation of Visual Culture Form and the Aesthetic Demand of the Public[J]. Film Literature, 2009(09):10-11.

an entertainment activity to relieve the stress of daily life, what the public expects is emotional relaxation from movies. As a result, more and more filmmakers have abandoned the field of art films and turned to cultivate the barren hills of commercial films. However, if we blindly cater to or satisfy the audience's aesthetic taste, it is easy to produce a batch of poor quality films, which not only disrupts the healthy development of the thriving film market, but also confuses the audience's aesthetic consciousness. It will definitely hinder the progress of the Chinese film industry. [53]The audience's expectation psychology is closely related to aesthetic needs, among which entertainment expectations, education needs, emotional transfer and experience are the most important aspects. [54]Audiences hope to obtain spiritual pleasure and sensory satisfaction when appreciating film and television works. When you want to change your mood when you are sad and disappointed after studying and working, and when you are bored, you can enjoy the relaxed and free aesthetic experience brought by film and television works, and temporarily put aside the troubles of reality. [55]People are eager to understand the outside world, obtain more information, and peep into other people's living conditions and inner secrets. However, with the development of society, there is less and less sincere communication between people, and the hearts become more and more separated. Due to the limitation of subjective and objective conditions, people's experience is limited. Therefore, film and television have become the best way for audiences to satisfy their curiosity and curiosity. Outside of work and life, people are eager to find an ideal spiritual world for emotional release, transfer and satisfaction. The art of film and television provides people with such an emotional space and spiritual realm. Whether the audience brings another side of themselves into their perception or brings their existing side into their emotions, it is all within the scope of the audience's self-acceptance.

Today's film and television companies, when promoting film and

---

[53] Cheng Wenguang. The Transformation of Visual Culture Form and the Aesthetic Demand of the Public[J]. Film Literature, 2009(09):10-11.

[54] Lei Meng. Warmth and Carnival: An Analysis of the Aesthetic Taste of Current Domestic Movie Audiences[J].Film Literature,2011(17):22-23.

[55] Liu Ying. Looking at the Expectation Psychology of Movie and TV Audiences from the Aesthetic Needs[J]. Film Literature, 2009(15):11-12.

television works to the public, first think of who will accept it, how many people will accept it, and the scope of acceptance, and then think of the value of the work itself, but we must know that this kind of Value is also judged by the audience. This is also the right of visual art to the audience for criticism. Because in this visual culture, the focus of the audience is the critical acceptance of images. Just as Yan Qianhai said in "Film and Television Literary Criticism": "Film and television, as a technical means, pays special attention to the novel experience of the recipients. The audience not only weakens the patience of literary works to a certain extent, but also raises questions about the film. Higher requirements and nitpicking of traditional films have led to the emergence of different film aesthetic standards." Movies are like this, TV dramas are a daily existence, and audiences are constantly improving their self-aesthetics. At the same time, they also have stricter aesthetics for the art of TV dramas Require.

CHAPTER FOUR THE ARTISTIC PRINCIPLES OF VISUAL FORMS OF TV DRAMAS

THE CONSTRUCTION OF VISUAL FORM UNDER THE FRAMEWORK OF GESTALT PSYCHOLOGY

People's conscious activities are objective and can be analyzed and studied through observation and practice, but the inner world of human beings, that is, emotion, perception, and thinking, is abstract. Based on this contradictory psychology of human beings, modern psychologists advocate Observable behavioral activity research, to explore the human mind, the most famous of which is the Gestalt theory's exploration of the human visual cognition mechanism. Gestalt has two meanings: one refers to shape or form, which is the actual nature of an object; the other refers to a specific object and the unique shape or form it has. This article is about combining Gestalt psychology with visual form. To put it simply, the visual form plays a vital role in TV dramas. When watching TV dramas, what people watch is the complete storyline, so how to impress the audience with a deep visual cognition requires the independent Plot elements are associated. The perceptual organization law in Gestalt psychology helps to integrate elements such as color, line, space, and form in the visual picture, and can focus the audience's attention on specific elements to achieve a specific expressive intention.[56]

The main content of the Gestalt includes visual unity, image and

---

[56] Pan Kewu. Mirror World – Visual Communication of TV Dramas [M]. Beijing: China Film Publishing House, 2010.11.

background, and the background is an invisible graphic: visual unity means that there is a harmony and integrity in the visual connection. When people observe something, they start from the whole. Although the elements that make up the vision exist independently, there is consistency between the elements, and there is a harmony and completeness in the visual connection; image and background It means that a person's perceptual field is always divided into two parts: graphics and background. Graphics are a gestalt, a prominent entity, and something we perceive. The background is something that has not yet been differentiated and sets off the figure. When people look at an object, they see the figure in an undifferentiated background, and the structure in the visual field is constantly changing. When the observed object and its background are observed on the same plane, there are also primary and secondary, not observed at the same time. At this time, once our attention is focused on the observed object, the background of the observed object will be different. in a secondary position. We often ignore the existence of the background, but it is precisely because of the composition of this element that the observed subject is more vivid and three-dimensional. Vision is an important means for people to obtain external information. Visually, people will actively group things with similar properties or characteristics into one category, such as the surface image, positional relationship, and color brightness of objects. For example, when people communicate with each other in life, in addition to the voice of the main body, there are environmental background sounds, but even so, we can clearly distinguish which sounds we need to receive and which are background sounds. We cannot ignore that background is an important element that makes up the integrity of something. The construction under the framework of Gestalt psychology can be divided into three parts: the external form of single screen - multi-screen, film and television visual blank space and gestalt psychology, psychological gestalt and the internal movement of visual form.

1. External form single screen - multi-screen

The world-renowned view of McLuhan, the master of the media environment school: "The medium is the message" made a note for the media technology to become an important driving force for communication, and then Paul Levinson's "Media Evolution Theory" made media technology an important fulcrum for communication. further solidified. According to the environmental school's point of view, at each stage of the development of the times, it is no longer the content that produces positive and beneficial information to society, but the carrier of dissemination of information, that is, the nature of the communication tool promotes the development of society. The form conversion from single screen to multi-screen is a technological breakthrough in information acquisition and information transmission. The result of this technological breakthrough is that people can obtain information more conveniently and quickly. It is specifically manifested in four points:

The first point is that different screen forms give people different psychological feelings. According to Gestalt psychology, people will have a psychological feeling that tends to be perfect in the process of pursuing things. In order to satisfy people's demand for perfection in understanding things, the process of turning imperfection into perfection is reflected in the information communication media, which is the form of single-screen to multi-screen communication tools.

The second point is in terms of form and content. Because of the different screens, whether it is a large screen or a small screen, vertical or horizontal screens, the changes in visual form tend to be diversified, which also satisfies the needs of people. The need for variety of things. In the media environment of "integrated media", TV dramas, as a unique program ecology, have slowly shifted their living environment from simple TV screens to PCs, tablets, and rapidly shifted to mobile phones, multimedia TVs and other integrated media platforms. The emergence of this phenomenon satisfies the diverse needs of the public and achieves a better communication effect than single-screen TV dramas. With the development of the times, the development of media technology has also comprehensively affected important links such as the creation, production, publicity and marketing of TV dramas. [57]In the face of strong market competition, the single TV drama broadcasting platform in the past can no longer meet the development needs of the industry. It is necessary to

---

[57] He Yan.Analysis of the Multidimensional Influence of the New Media Ecology on the Creation of TV Dramas[J].China Television,2018(06):12-17.

achieve industrial upgrading and a diversified marketing model to gain a foothold in the industry.

The third point, this change from single screen to multi-screen, the most important point is to increase the function of instant messaging. Compared with traditional television communication tools, people focus on receiving information. However, the application of mobile phones and tablets has achieved the release of instant messaging, that is, the seamless connection of receiving and releasing, which brings great convenience and perfect feeling to the audience when receiving and sending information. What this change perfects is The self-soothing function of the audience.

The last point is that the development of technology has brought about an increase in the rate of information transmission. When this information transmission rate continues to increase, one of the results is actually information overload. The multi-screen communication tool alleviates the negative impact of information overload, and the emergence of such a variety of platforms reduces the anxiety brought about by information overload. The positive phenomenon it produces is not only to accept the perfection of information, but also to reduce the imperfection of information, and it also turns information dissemination into a variety of forms of cooperation. The wave of mobile Internet promotes the rise of mobile terminals, and more and more users begin to wander among various terminals such as TVs, computers, smart phones, and tablets. This change affects people's lives in a subtle way, and even touches the In various fields and industries, the "screens" that used to perform their duties have also begun to cooperate across platforms. In this era of multi-screen communication, multi-terminal and multi-screen interactive Unicom has become the general trend. Online viewing or offline downloading viewing modes such as computers, tablets, and mobile phones no longer have an impact on traditional TV screen playback platforms. is a shock. The advancement of the network environment, the popularity of smart portable terminals, even watches and glasses have become the "multi-screen era" of Internet mobile terminals, and the seamless connection between screens is becoming a new consumer hotspot.[58]

With the passing of the century, there have been two important shifts

---

[58] Jin Yuxi, Bu Yanfang. Multi-screen Interactive Strategy of TV Media in the Mobile Internet Era[J]. China Radio and Television Journal, 2015(10):65-67.

in the visual focus of TV audiences: first, in the first ten years of the century, TV audiences shifted from watching TV in the living room to PC terminals relying on the Internet, and audiences are accustomed to The timeliness and interactivity of computer-based video interaction. The second time was from 2010 to 2018. The viewing habits of TV audiences shifted to mobile Internet media, and they began to enjoy movies through mobile media such as tablets and mobile phones. In the context of new media, TV dramas appear on video websites, portal websites, WeChat, and Weibo, and begin to enter the stage of integration with new media.[59]

2. Visual blank space and Gestalt psychology in film and television

Gestalt psychology, also called Gestalt psychology, its core content is the principle of integrity. While Gestalt psychology integrates experience and behavior, it believes that the whole is not the sum of its parts, and to some extent it is greater than the sum of its parts. Therefore, we should use the overall structural view when studying psychological phenomena. People's cognition of things has a natural tendency towards perfection. Under different perceptions such as vision, hearing and touch, when they feel incomplete or imperfect, human consciousness will automatically supplement this imperfection. At this time we regard the act of consciousness as the impetus of a force which stimulates the imperfection in the psychic change from imperfection to perfection. According to the definition of psychological gestalt, it is not difficult to see that psychological gestalt and TV dramas based on visual forms have essentially similar aspects on the artistic level.

The application of the artistic technique of "leaving blank" in traditional Chinese culture and the aesthetic imagery of "combining virtual and real" in my country's film and television art works has produced its unique artistic value and charm. The concept of blank space in Chinese film and television dramas not only runs through the artistic ideas of "turning emptiness into a realm" and "turning emptiness into reality" in classical aesthetics, but also expands its scope of meaning, from picture

---

[59] Sun Hongyu. Fragmented Narrative Tendency of TV Documentaries under the Background of Media Convergence[J]. Film Review, 2014(18):86-87.

processing, sound performance to actors' lines and Performance, from the expression of narrative time and space to the implementation of narrative strategies, is manifested in all aspects of art forms. In fact, the law of blank space starts from the audience's acceptance psychology and grasps three lines: concise and focused narrative style, aesthetic artistic expression, and narrative method full of curiosity and expectation. Among them, there is an artistic conception that is in line with the aesthetics of traditional Chinese culture, such as tranquility, far-reaching, and profound meaning; at the same time, it also meets the needs of the concise, ups and downs of the plot development of the current film and television media art. It combines traditional thinking with modern ideas, and adds to the artistic concept of aesthetics. Such a change makes the film and television media art more in line with the public's aesthetic taste, and also makes the art of film and television works have a higher artistic value.

In the traditional Chinese concept of art, "nothing" is produced on the basis of "something", and "you" sets off the existence of "nothing". Without "you", there is no "nothing". " is attached to "being", but "nothing" also occupies an important position in artistic expression, such as the "blank" technique in the art of Chinese painting creation. From the perspective of creative skills, it is precisely because of the role of blank space that the vivid image of the subject is vivid on the paper, and at the same time, the composition of the entire artwork is simple and clear, and the theme is clear. For example, Qi Baishi's shrimps and Xu Beihong's horses highlight that there are no other complicated objects outside the subject, and gather the public's attraction on the subject of the painting, while the environment where the subject is located is constructed by the public's blank psychology. Graphic art still has the technique of blank space, and dynamic film and television works of art will also use blank space to the extreme. From the perspective of the overall tone of the film, the use of blank space can not only play a role in transitioning the plot of the film and inspiring the audience's emotions, but also control the rhythm and tone of the entire work, and better convey the creator's intention of. Giving the art of "blank space" to the screen of film and television works gives the audience the power to judge, and virtually achieves the emotional communication between the creator and the audience.

In works of film and television art creation, from the perspective of expression skills, lens language, music sound, and color shading all involve the use of blank space. From the perspective of film emotional tone, the emotional changes of the audience can also be realized with the art of blank space. The "blank space" of the screen in film and television works is mainly realized by using film and television languages such as lens, composition, light and shadow, and color. The technique of film and television blank space has the following aspects: screen blank, music blank, and narrative blank.

The "blank space" of the screen is most often expressed in the form of empty shots in film and television works. The so-called empty shot literally means that there is no one there. Professionally speaking, it is a shot with only scenery and no portraits. The creators have elevated the use of empty shots to a professional skill, because empty shots can not only express the creator's emotional intentions, but also give the audience a sense of the creator's intentions across time and space. At the same time, in terms of technique, the empty shot also completes the transition of the scene very well.

The music blank conveys the artistic conception of "silence is better than sound at this time". This kind of artistic conception is the commanding height of emotional catharsis. This kind of use has been reflected in Chinese poems as early as, such as "Look at each other forever, only Jingting Mountain" and Su Shi's "Looking at each other without words, only a thousand lines of tears ", have made a very good interpretation of the use of this music blank space. As a kind of audio-visual art work, TV dramas are only for visual aesthetics. It also plays a role that cannot be ignored. If a film and television work is filled with background music from the beginning to the end, not only does it not have the effect of icing on the cake, but it affects the viewing experience of the entire film.

In film and television works, the traditional narrative structure is often based on the timeline or the development of the storyline. Narrative blanks generally create a kind of suspense through the absence of important plot clues. Simply put, it is used to strengthen the suspense of the film. a creative method. Another way of expressing the blankness of the narrative is to set an open ending, leaving an unclear ending so as to leave the audience with more room for thinking and individual interpretation. This suspense-setting narrative structure is more in line with the "continuity principle" of Gestalt psychology. From this point of view, creators want to use the art of blank space in film and television works, which is necessarily related to the audience's gestalt psychology. At the same time, the education level of the audience is also closely related to the perception and experience of the media cultivated in the process of life.[60]

3. Mental Gestalt and the inner movement of visual forms

The dynamic expression methods that constitute the visual form include montage, motion lens, editing and so on. The language of the shot is composed of comprehensive elements such as the scene, the angle of the shooting picture, the orientation of the subject, and the way the camera moves. The combination and patchwork of the shots are important factors that affect the integrity of the film. Moving shots can better meet the audience's visual beauty needs than freeze-frame images. Every movement of the camera can not only show the characteristics of the subject, but also introduce the relationship between multiple subjects, interpret the emotional expression of the characters and introduce the overall environment. etc., bringing the audience a unique visual form experience.

To grasp the relationship between psychological gestalt and the internal movement of visual form, this article takes montage as a representative to further explain. When montage is applied to film and television art works, what it presents is that when different lens groups are connected together, they often produce meanings that each lens does not have when it exists alone. In other words, when the independent shots are spliced together, in addition to carrying their own independent narrative content, they will produce different narrative content, which can achieve unexpected visual effects, thereby further forming the core of the film. integrity. Just as Eisenstein's point of view: "We have already pointed out that what is combined in the montage is not some details in essence, but countless general concepts about things or phenomena produced by the details according to the local law of representing the whole. Therefore, what is contained in the montage combination is not just the sum of details

---

[60] Zhang Pan.Aesthetic Analysis of Blank Space in Film and Television[J].Film Literature,2008(14):24.

composed of various elements forming a static whole of the sum, but something much larger. It is not the sum of five details forming a whole, it is five There are two whole numbers, each of which is taken from another perspective and another aspect, and all of them are mutually inclusive." [61] In summary, we can draw the conclusion that the relationship between the whole and the part of montage art is the same as that of completeness. The core issues of type psychology are similar.

Montage can be roughly divided into narrative montage and expressive montage. The function of narrative montage is to tell the storyline of film and television works, and expressive montage is the sublimation of narrative montage, so it is more aesthetically appealing. The use of montage in film and television shows the creator's subjective intention, which has obvious directionality and guidance. Part of the information received by the audience is what the creator wants to express, and part of it is the audience's self-perception under the montage art. This montage technique is called rational expression.

Metaphor montage in performance montage has always been controversial, but it is an important way of expression in film and television works. Metaphor montage implicitly and vividly expresses a certain meaning of the creator through the comparison of shots or scenes. This technique presents the similar characteristics of different things in a paragraph in the form of comparison, so as to arouse the audience's association, understand the meaning of the director, and express a strong emotional appeal. By using metaphor montage to reassemble shots, paragraphs, and scenes, the creator can guide the audience's attention and stimulate the audience's association. The emotional expression and recognition of this metaphor in different things needs to rely on the audience's Gestalt mental ability. This kind of visual perception ability directly affects the quality of the creator's use of metaphor montage in film and television works. That is to say, the audience's overall grasp of film and television works is the key to judging whether a film has artistic value. If the creator's subjective image does not agree with the audience's acceptance concept, it will affect the effect of the whole work. Therefore, in the process of using metaphor montage, creators should follow the "proximity or proximity principle" and "similarity principle " of the perceptual organization principle of Gestalt psychology.

---

[61] Eisenstein. On Montage [M]. Beijing: China Film Press, 2003.

VISUAL FORM

The staged characteristics of the development of visual form include the "inorganic form" of primitive art, the "organic form" of classical art, the "inorganic form" of modern art and the "formless" of postmodern art. This staged feature of visual form is restricted by the social development conditions and the development background of the times, and it is also inseparable from the changes in human psychology and the development and evolution of art itself.

"Inorganic forms" (geometric shapes) in primitive society: Perception and comprehension of visual forms appeared in the primitive society period, but due to the development of social productivity level, objects in the primitive period paid more attention to its practicability, and at the same time were influenced by primitive social science Restricted by technology, human beings respect nature and admire witchcraft, the characteristics of art in the primitive period are generally symmetry, repetition and rhythm. The presentation of this form is the result of understanding the external environment.

The "organic form" of classical art (decoration of plants, animals, etc.): During this period, human beings gradually shifted from slave society to agricultural society and developed into industrial society. Although society has undergone great changes in terms of class and social functions, there has not been much change in the form of visual art. The handicrafts in the period of agricultural society to a large extent reflect the characteristics of the era of agricultural society, that is, the close relationship between man and nature. Since the industrial society is a rational, organized and disciplined society, the basic characteristics of the combination with visual art are: standardization, modelization, and practicality, so what is reflected in the visual form is the value attribute of commodities and practical value.

The "inorganic form" (geometric shape) of modern art: the "inorganic form" of primitive art and the "organic form" of classical art are similar under the aesthetic standard of visual form, and they both show the symmetry of structure, Ratio's standardized identity and unity. But the "inorganic form" of modern art has gradually broken this unified standard model, presenting a variety of visual forms. In terms of the characteristics of the visual form itself, this period was influenced by Cubism, Dadaism, and Surrealism. The traditional rules of form were gradually eliminated, and new and diversified forms were accepted. This change is closely related to the development of the times, and is inseparable from the changes in the public's aesthetic taste. In the 1960s, the voices of art and society to express themselves and pursue the liberation of their own individuality became louder and louder. People began to question the possibility and rationality of rationality, and then began to think about the meaning and value of human existence. And other issues—corresponding to the field of visual art, the integrity, normative, and systematic visual form norms are broken up and reconstructed, so the visual form transitions to the next period.[62]

"Formless" of post-modern art (coexistence of various forms): Post-modern art concepts advocate pluralism and oppose rationalism and authoritative concepts. Post-modern art has developed to this period, and it has questioned rational concepts in industrial society, while conforming to the ideological trend of the times, the concept of art forms tends to be diverse and diverse, and the aesthetic concept of art that coexists in various forms is highly respected. Correspondingly, the art of this period is highly decorative in terms of visual form and external expression characteristics, opposing standards and patterns, and its internal theory shows a sense of formlessness, so there will be absurdity, ridicule, and jokes and a sense of humor. "Postmodern art and culture is not only about the aestheticization of objects and images, it has also successfully avoided some of the shortcomings of commercialization; in this sense, it is both radical and conservative, both avant-garde and mixed. Integration". On the other hand, postmodern visual art also pays attention to non-visual sensory experience, such as touch, smell, taste and other elements, which are not included in traditional visual art forms, but with the advancement of technology of the times, these elements Visibility is gradually formed. From this aspect, the visual art form is expanded from the content field.

1. Heteronomy and Autonomy of Visual Form

Generally speaking, the visual perception based on the natural factors of seeing is autonomous, while the perception supplemented by other non-visual factors is heteronomy. Heteronomy and autonomy of visual form,

---

[62] Cao Hui. Gu Pengfei. Overview of Visual Forms [J]. Literary Review. 2006.

form is content. Generally speaking, the visual perception based on the natural factors of seeing is autonomous, while the perception supplemented by other non-visual factors is heteronomy. The so-called self-discipline means that we no longer follow the given reality and start to construct independently. There are two situations in daily viewing: first, when facing a viewing object, visual perception occurs through simple viewing without the intervention of other non-visual information, such as facing a person who has never seen before. Second, a visual object is perceived only with the intervention of other non-visual information, such as facing a familiar object or having other backgrounds even when facing it for the first time Sex information assistance. That is to say, its visual perception cannot depend on other non-visual factors, and the self-discipline of visual form has two levels of regulations: first, it is related to images, which can be said to be the perception of graphics and colors. etc.; secondly, it cannot be connected with what is intended to be given. This pre-given image perception can be perceptual or tactile. [63]Therefore, we say that the key to the self-discipline of visual forms is not whether to use images, but how to use them. Of course, in the face of any image, our visual perception will not be purely determined by vision, we will have our own vision and perceptual thinking, so vision cannot be autonomous and heteronomy; A visual form, people will always inject some meaning into it, the so-called reading is actually this injection. For humans, form always has content and conveys something. Therefore, forms cannot be self-disciplined, they are all heteronomy, and heteronomy comes from other non-visual factors. Based on the above, we can know that the autonomy and heteronomy of visual forms make visual perception have different uniqueness and conventionability. The autonomous form is based on the independent construction of meaning by perceptuality. It is unique because there is no intervention of perception and rational activities. It is not unique because people have the same perceptual activities; On the basis of meaning, it is not unique because other non-perceptual connotations penetrate into the perceptual form, and it is unique because non-perceptual activities such as perception or rationality are not the same among people. The commensurability of the autonomic form points to the spontaneous

---

[63] Wang Caiyong. The Problem of Visual Form Autonomy and Visual Modernity[J]. Qiushi Academic Journal, 2014,41(06):20-26.

common characteristics at the level of perception, while the covenantability of the heteronomous form points to the recoverable intellectual or rational content in perceptual activities, which can often be separated from the perceptual form and reside in the In other non-perceptual forms, such as categories, concepts, etc. The uniqueness and covenatability of different levels make the forms of self-discipline and heteronomy have completely different cultural connotations. [64]Generally speaking, self-discipline emphasizes "self", which is a kind of spontaneous and perceptual activity, and the weakening of rationality makes self-discipline transition to a barbaric nature. Heteronomy focuses on "he", which is a form that tends to inject perception and rationality. If there is no other sense involved, it is self-discipline, and if there is, it is heteronomy. We can clearly see that self-discipline and heteronomy are opposite. Therefore, for the autonomy and heteronomy of visual forms, we focus on the aspect of autonomy.

2. Form

The concepts in each of us are obtained from forms. Different forms can express different concepts, and the same form can also express different concepts. This shows that all kinds of abstract thinking produced by the brain are acted on the form, and the concept of the mind is obtained in the form. Therefore, we say that once the human brain has abstract thinking, the concept will be replaced by the form. no longer exists. Perception, language, communication, hallucinations, types and categories. The development of science and technology has promoted the change of people's communication tools, and the emergence of printing technology has contributed to the change of communication methods. People's communication methods have begun to replace face-to-face language communication with words. The visual cultural symbols gradually replaced the auditory sound culture in the primitive society where sound was the main face-to-face communication in the society. In film art, film is not a plastic art, but an expression of poetry, because film can absorb infinitely rich and colorful materials and transform them into non-image elements.

---

[64] Wang Caiyong. The Problem of Visual Form Autonomy and Visual Modernity[J]. Qiushi Academic Journal, 2014,41(06):20-26.

Like dreams, movies affect and synthesize sensations. Jones believes that the freedom of film is not only derived from space, but also from time. He said: "Movies are thoughts expressed through sound and sound. These thoughts are poured out in a continuous, rapidly changing image. The film is as clear as our thoughts, and the film speed is accompanied by flashbacks. The memory recalled, the quickness of the intentional change of the film is comparable to our thinking. The film has the rhythm of thinking flow, has the ability to change freely in time and space,... What the film projects is pure thought, pure dream, Pure inner life." [65]Visual art is changing its form at any time, making form a means of artistic expression with strong personality. The visual art formed also has the characteristics of strong language symbols, which connect people's perception and images, and standardize the basis of visual art. Visual language has become the most important way of language communication in today's society. Its unique language symbol has become a necessary means to beautify life and improve the quality of life.[66]

"The so-called form refers to the equal function of the physical form and the psychological form, that is, the internal form can express the function of the external form. Or express the relationship between the external form and the internal form, and become a form." We regard form as the function of internal emotion. Self-expression, combined with the original state of the external form, the combination of the two forms the connotation of the form. [67]Significant forms refer to the visual art works created by creators, whether they are two-dimensional paintings or three-dimensional sculptures and buildings, all of which are endowed with different emotions by the creators. These works are the emotional output of the creators, and they are also the intentional expressions of the creators' emotions. When these works are completed and released to the public, they will bring the viewers an emotion similar to the creation of the creators or after the viewers watch them, they will be derived by themselves. out of emotion. This kind of emotion is a two-way expression, and we call this two-way communication aesthetic emotion. The details of

---

[65] 【US】Susan Lange. Liu Daji. Emotion and Form [M]. Fu Zhiqiang, Zhou Faxiang, translation. Beijing: China Social Sciences Press, 1986.8.

[66] Qian Jiayu. Visual Psychology [M]. Shanghai: Xuelin Publishing House. 2006.1.

[67] Qian Jiayu. Visual Psychology [M]. Shanghai: Xuelin Publishing House. 2006.1.

each part of these works, such as lines, colors, etc., constitute the unique artistic characteristics of the work itself, so this is our unique cognition and unique emotion for the attributes of the work. All of these combined together, we call "significant form". A good work of visual art will bring a person who can appreciate it to the pleasure outside of life, using art as a means to experience the emotions of life.[68]

3. Form: beauty with meaning

The word "form" in the Encyclopaedia Britannica broadly encompasses essential internal provisions in philosophy, literature, and the visual arts. "It only takes a brief glance at the history of aesthetics to know the importance of form theory." It [69]is not difficult to see the ontological position of form in aesthetics, and the reason why we call art art is that "form" makes them Be artistic. [70]The problem of form is rooted in the context of the development and evolution of German art history and aesthetic thought since modern times. After Kant's point of view, form is endowed with the concept of perception, so form is also related to the way people perceive the world. Academic trends such as psychology, positivism, cultural (spiritual) science, and neo-Kantianism have provided a hotbed for the development of art history science. Riegl and Wölfflin explored the inherent laws and laws of human visual form creation activities through the analysis of works and experiences. This academic concept and method of art history led to the discovery of the diachronic continuation and synchronic consistency of the visual form tradition, which strengthened people's awareness of the link between the independent and self-sufficient life process of the visual form and the spiritual life, and inspired such traditions and visual forms. New thinking on the relationship between national spirits.[71]

---

[68] [English] Bell. Art [M]. Xue Hua, translated. Nanjing: Jiangsu Education Press, 2004.8.

[69] 【English】Lee Stowell, Commentary on the History of Modern Aesthetics[M]. Jiang Kongyang, translated. Shanghai Translation Publishing House, 1980. pp. 188-189.

[70] Cao Hui. Aesthetic Research on Visual Forms--A Survey of Visual Forms Based on Western Visual Art [M]. Beijing: People's Publishing House, 2009.3.

[71] Zhang Jian. The Life of Visual Forms [M]. Hangzhou: China Academy of Art Press. 2004.7.

Form is a meaningful beauty, just as we know that beauty is a kind of artistic conception, and the expression of beauty requires symbol expression, so form becomes the main expression form of symbols, and symbols reach people, that is, forms are understood by people, People have new feelings of beauty, so form is beauty with meaning. And its significance lies in the docking of form and beauty. We call this kind of beauty of form. The beauty of form is the beauty of the form of a realistic image or an artistic image. It is not without content. It is a major feature of being connected with certain content but not completely relying on content. Belinsky Said: "If the form is the expression of the content, it must be closely related to the content. If you want to separate it from the content, it means to eliminate the content; the reverse is also the same: if you want to separate the content from the form, that is tantamount to eliminating the form." [72] As Hegel said, "the content is not the other, that is, the form is transformed into the content; the form is not the other, that is, the content is transformed into the form." [73]

As a comprehensive art form, film is also one of the classifications of visual film and television works. Regardless of the content of the film, the artistic value of the film, and the way of communication, the expression methods are various and different. of. But it is worth mentioning that the visual expression plays an important role in the content of the movie. For example, the scene setting of the movie, the picture effect, the control of the rhythm when composing the picture, and the scheduling of various scenes are all for the audience to experience. It is a key way to savor the environment carefully and feel the aesthetics in terms of form and content. The visual expression of movies can be seen from two aspects: on the one hand, the visual expression process of movies can be divided into different screen displays within a certain period of time., information feedback, and then get a sense of beauty in the spirit in this series of processes; on the other hand, the visual expression process of movies can also be regarded as switching between different visual pictures, and comparing with different visual pictures, in the audience's eyes. The visual plot displayed by the

---

[72] 【Su】Belinsky. Belinsky's Literature [M]. Liang Zhen, translated. New Literature and Art Publishing House. 1958.7.
[73] Georg Wilhelm Friedrich Hegel. Small logic [M]. Shanghai People's Publishing House. 1817.

visual flow of the picture is produced in the thought, and the perfect display of the visual plot assists the conveyance and expression of the film's ideological content and spiritual connotation. From the above two aspects, the shaping of the aesthetic feeling in every visual picture of the movie is essential. [74]This is the feeling of the beauty of form brought to us by the visual form of movies. Similarly, in the visual form of TV dramas, visual expression is also a manifestation of beauty: TV dramas are extended versions of movies that are close to reality, relying on imagination and visual perception. The final product presented in artistic form, visual form. For TV dramas, different abstract forms determine different visual effects. By referring to and inheriting the aesthetic concepts and creative techniques of film art, I can show the personality characteristics that I want to express in my works.

4. Form as Symbol: Aesthetic Expression with Meaningful Interaction

Form is a kind of beauty with meaning, but we know that symbols are the manifestations of forms. Therefore, what we are going to discuss is how the form as a symbol, that is, the form itself as the manifestation of other things, expresses aesthetic ideas. To understand this, we need to know what the symbol is? On the one hand, understanding a symbol is a simple, diverse but widely used mark or mark used to express a certain meaning, such as our common punctuation marks or mathematical symbols; in manifestation. The relationship between symbols and meanings is complex. Symbols are a form of expression for our understanding of meaning. For example, when we mention "chopsticks", we think of eating. Symbols subtly connect our perception with the meaning expressed by the symbols, and we will form this connection in our consciousness to make relevant reactions. There is an academic theory-semiotics on the discussion of signs for signs. Semiotics is a theory that first appeared in the West in the 19th century. In different backgrounds, it has been divided into two different parts after different analyzes and discussions. One is the anthropology represented by Cahill Susan. In the symbolic semiotics of development, in

---

[74] Li Yan. Film Screen Composition and Visual Form Beauty Principles[J].Film Literature,2007(24):8-9.

her opinion, symbols are created by people. With the development of the times and the progress of society, people's awareness of symbols is getting higher and higher. Cassirer believes that people are also symbols. One, is a symbol with an active behavior. All human behaviors are symbols conveyed as active symbols. Simply speaking, people are a kind of symbol, and human behavior is also a symbol, and the core and root of all these, and the core of the core is the symbol; except Cassirer's This theoretical cognition, and another is the semiotics of structuralism derived from structuralism. They strive to find an innovative way for linguistics from the perspective of scientificity and accuracy. We can analyze the culture and art of society from different angles, and the emergence of semiotics has opened up a new perspective for us to observe. Semioticians propose that all rational or perceptual behaviors of people and the development and inheritance of culture of people in social development need the help of symbols, which may be in the form of language, characters or any other a form of expression. The existence of art is a special form of expression that integrates various emotions, culture, and knowledge. Art has also become a product of history in the long river of history. Therefore, in general, any symbol is a discipline with expressive significance that is generated interactively between human self-consciousness and social experience.

Symbols have common characteristics: people always have a long-standing wish in the long river of history, just like from ancient times to the present, ancient emperors have been seeking the prescription of immortality, and now people work hard to learn and struggle just to enjoy life better, But the premise of enjoyment is to have a healthy body. Therefore, joy and well-being become the most lasting and eternal desire. Therefore, such a demand has become a common ideal symbol for everyone. It is the so-called commonality of symbols. This commonality comes from the common cultural cognition of everyone. Although life experiences are different, they all have the same appeal.

Symbols have the characteristics of transcendence: it is precisely because people have desires and ideals that they can be full of passion for life, life can continue, and society can develop under human activities. Symbols have a strong transcendence. With the development of life and the progress of society, symbols, as a form of expression, have a performance beyond the previous ones in both content and form.

Symbols have the characteristics of simplicity: the most essential difference between symbols and other art forms is the simplicity and simplicity of symbols. It is not as complicated as professional art, but it is a popular art form that is more acceptable to the public. Whether it is the traditional meaning of ancient culture or the modern popular form, it is simple and intuitive. This kind of simplicity is not only the work itself, but also the simplicity and easy-to-understand under the symbolic expression. For example, our sculpture art is pure in terms of color, and the composition materials and the creator's intention to express are more distinct. This is simplicity as a symbol of popular art form.

The symbol has the characteristics of perfection: Although the public has different feelings about aesthetics, everyone likes to agree with good looks. Generally speaking, it is good-looking. Symbols are no exception. Modeling symbols give people a perfect and complete feeling in their internal composition and external image expression. A symbol is complete in itself, a living, unified thing. Second, no matter what form the combination of symbols is made of, whether single or complex, they are all complete, so when forming symbols, they are a complete unity. Of course, there are also various and complex modeling methods, such as the integrity of the freehand method, the fantasy of the realistic method, etc., all have different ways of changing. Modeling symbols, no matter what form of expression,

After reading the commonality, transcendence, simplicity, and perfection of symbols, we can draw such a conclusion that symbols can be a specific carrier or form of information, an important element of information dissemination, or an abstract consciousness Performance. We can classify symbols into two categories: one is linguistic symbols, and the other is non-linguistic symbols. And what we want to discuss is form as a symbol, which is the same as what we mentioned above "form is the expression of symbols, and when symbols reach people, people have a feeling of beauty, and beauty is expressed by symbols, so it is Formed a kind of interaction, which is the interactive expression of the feeling of beauty." The strengthening of this statement, the form as a symbol, that is, the form is expressed to people in the form of symbols, so that people can accept a specific expression Or the externalized form makes people obtain a kind of artistic conception, which is also a kind of aesthetics. The form conveyed to people as an external symbol becomes the connection between the two, the combination of meaning and beauty, thus achieving a kind of interactivity.

The Frenchman Metz was the first to introduce semiotics into film and television studies, and he described Hollywood movies as a semiotic system. We collectively refer to film and television art as film and television art. As an artistic symbol, it acts on many aspects and influences each other. One is its image function. This kind of image is the product of adding subjective intentions to objective things from different angles by relying on the pictures of the camera. When we refer to an objective thing, it is the image reflection of the thing in our imagination;, Image symbols evoke our previous reflections on things with intuitive images, so this is a two-way process, a process of acceptance and projection; the third is the symbolic function, which is brought into the abstract process with intuitive and concrete images.

Generally speaking, the aesthetic value of images depends on the diversity of symbols. As a symbol, the form of visual art has an aesthetic expression. Diderot attributed beauty to the feeling of relationship, and placed the concept of relationship in the abstraction of things by the understanding. Therefore, comprehension's investigation of the relationship among things is a kind of rational cognition, and the pleasure brought by beauty comes after the concept of relationship is aroused in human's comprehension. The people here are defined by Diderot as "creatures whose physical and mental structures are like ours", not individual people. In this way, after solving the problem of the root of beauty, Diderot gave beauty a universal rational basis, and at the same time emphasized the psychological effect of beauty. Although we have various factors (Didero listed twelve sources of disagreement about beauty, such as human intellectual ability, experience, custom, talent, upbringing, age, prejudice, etc.) that affect our judgment, we cannot deny that beauty It is the feeling that resides in the relationship.[75]

---

[75] Du Wei. Diderot's Aesthetic Thought from the Theory of "Beauty in Relationship" [D]. Shanghai Normal University, 2015.

5. The Combination of Western Logical Aesthetics and Eastern Philosophy

The history of western logic mainly includes the development of formal logic and inductive logic in western history. The history of Western logic was born in the period of ancient Greece and Rome. The logic of the ancient Greek period was the beginning of the history of Western logic, and it developed greatly in the period of Aristotle. He is a master in the development of Western logic history, and has promoted the development direction of logical thought system, and built a perfect logical thought system. [76]And the development of logical thought in the Middle Ages has gone through transition, creation and perfection stages. The beginning of the Renaissance stage is when logical thinking entered the modern period, when humanistic logic aroused the thinking and reflection of scholars. Modern logic puts forward new propositions at the current stage of development, namely mathematical logic and modern inductive logic, and deals with logical problems in a mathematical thinking theory mode, which is a new direction for the development of logical thinking. Western logic aesthetics is the aesthetics of formal logic and inductive logic. Western logic was founded by Aristotle. His core logic first took deductive logic as its core content and focused on deductive methods as its main feature. Western logic aesthetics is the aesthetics of formal logic and inductive logic.

So what is aesthetics? This issue has been interpreted differently in the course of China's development. The concept of aesthetics was first introduced to China by Japan in the 20th century. Mr. Wang Guowei, a Chinese scholar, believes that the most fundamental characteristic of aesthetics is not because it is a part of the philosophy system, but because Aesthetics is a layer of rationality added to aesthetics, not just intuitive views and thinking. Provide some kind of "beauty standard" for life, so that people can reasonably lead to the ideal path. The beauty he thinks can be divided into sublime and beautiful, and the distinction between the two is related to the relationship between this thing and me and my attitude towards this thing. Contrary to Mr. Wang Guowei's viewpoint, Zong Baihua, a famous master of aesthetics, believes that

---

[76] Mao Conghu et al. History of European Philosophy [M]. Tianjin: Nankai University Press, 1985.

"everything about the cultural world, the spiritual world, and the beauty of the whole world belongs to aesthetics. That is, art is also a part of aesthetics, but art Although it is a part of aesthetics, its content is not limited to aesthetics." [77]He subtracted the discussion of creation methods and structures from aesthetics, endowed aesthetics with a philosophical nature, and strengthened the status of aesthetics as a branch of philosophy. As many scholars will consider this point, as part of the philosophy of aesthetics history, scholar Zhu Guangqian also believes that "aesthetics" mainly discusses "beauty", and art is a highly concentrated embodiment of "beauty", so the study of art It is the central question in the study of aesthetics. In his view, although aesthetics is based on the theory of philosophy, philosophy is the foundation of aesthetics, and the development of aesthetics is based on philosophy. At the same time, aesthetics has its own development field in the category of philosophy. However, if it is not enough to analyze the basis of aesthetics from a scientific point of view, then we need to use psychological methods. Aesthetics is different from philosophy and can make scientific judgments and choices on rational cognition. Therefore, what we cannot ignore is The role of psychological factors in the study of aesthetics. Of course, in Cai Yi's view, aesthetics is aesthetics, and it is his own independent art discipline, which is not equal to art science. Aesthetics is a discipline system based on the study of art., but there is an essential difference between aesthetics and art, and he does not believe that aesthetics can be equated with psychology. He believes that aesthetics includes three parts, namely, realistic beauty, aesthetic feeling, and art. He believes that aesthetics is the aesthetics of philosophy, the application of philosophy in the field of aesthetics, and a kind of epistemology.

Then there was Li Zehou's understanding of aesthetics: the beauty of art is always an important factor for art to be art, but art is by no means equal to the beauty of art. He believes that aesthetics includes three aspects: the philosophical theory of beauty, the psychology of aesthetics, and the society of art. In the 1990s, a group of scholars called "post-practical aesthetics" had their own opinions on aesthetics research. Yang Chunshi, one of the representatives, regarded aesthetics as the way of life of personal

[77] Zong Baihua. The Complete Works of Zong Baihua: Volume One [M]. Hefei: Anhui Education Press, 1994.

freedom, that is, "aesthetics". Aesthetic consciousness is rooted in people's "non-consciousness", which is a complex psychological structure operation process. In fact, not only these scholars, but also many scholars have continuously discussed and revised "what is aesthetics" in the development history of our country, but combining all the academic knowledge and our discussion of form symbols above, we can know that beauty is a This kind of artistic conception is symbolized, and this symbol is accepted by people, and we humans have a feeling of beauty, which is another artistic conception. Therefore, in Western logic aesthetics, when we symbolize logic to the public, the public will have a feeling of artistic conception for the received logic, forming an interactive aesthetic feeling.

Eastern philosophy refers to Indian philosophy, Chinese philosophy, Korean philosophy, Japanese philosophy, etc. It discusses the science of the most general and universal laws of nature, human society, and human thinking itself. The core issues are still the basic issues of thinking and existence. The development of Eastern philosophy reveals the struggles and discussions among different factions in various periods. Of course, the history of Eastern philosophy also has its own characteristics. As Ren Houkui said in his "A Brief Introduction to Eastern Philosophy": First, the content of Eastern philosophy Rich. What we have to admit is that the East has experienced a long period of time in ancient society, so the different philosophical arguments produced in different periods are more colorful; secondly, Eastern philosophy is an inherited philosophical system. From the ancient oriental motto "respect the teacher and respect the Tao", we can know that the inheritance of Confucianism in our country still occupies a large part of our life; moreover, Eastern philosophy is a theoretical form closely related to religion. The earliest yin and yang and the five elements in China show that the philosophies of various countries were born out of embracing religion; then, Eastern philosophy focuses on the study of life. No matter whether it is exploring heaven and man, name and reality, ancient and modern, it is inseparable from the subject of man, and the study of man's norms, moral norms, life happiness, etc.; finally, Eastern philosophy has a strong tendency of irrationalism. Irrationalism emphasizes introspective, intuitive personal experience.

After knowing what is Western Logical Aesthetics and Eastern Philosophy, for the combination of the two, we know that philosophy needs to use logic to provide accurate and powerful analysis, and because aesthetics is a branch of philosophy, logical aesthetics is also included in philosophy It also gives a philosophical and rational analysis. The two complement each other, are different from each other and are related to each other.

VISUAL FORMS OF TV DRAMAS

The visual form of TV dramas is the psychological activity associated with human beings and vision. These psychological activities are finally presented in a certain artistic form and visual style through the complex psychological activities of the creative subject and the receiving subject. The visual form of TV dramas and the presentation of visual forms on images are the key factors that determine the visual expression and dissemination of TV dramas. [78]In a nutshell, the visual form of TV dramas is an art form that combines human visual information and psychological activities. Visual form is essentially an abstract thinking mode, and visual form is also an important theoretical basis for TV drama creation. The visual form of TV dramas is the psychological activity associated with vision. These psychological activities are finally presented in a certain artistic form and visual form through the complex psychological activities of the creative subject and the receiving subject. The visual form of TV dramas and the presentation of visual forms on images are the key factors that determine the visual expression and dissemination of TV dramas. For TV drama reception, the audience is actively participating in the perception process provided by the abstract form in the TV drama in an intuitive way during the visual process. The thinking is transformed from image to abstract or from abstract to image, and the perception recognizes the unique form. artistic enjoyment. For the creation of TV dramas, the figurative things are very limited, but the abstract things are infinite. It can be said that there are as many visual effects as there are abstract forms. Therefore, in the creation and reception of TV dramas, the infinite potential of human creativity is reflected in the multiple possibilities of abstract forms. The

---

[78] Pan Kewu.On the Visual Form of TV Drama[J].Modern Communication-Journal of Communication University of China,2009.4.15.

visual form opens up the imaginary world of TV series. [79]In the process of watching TV dramas, the audience needs to combine the combined effects of vision, hearing and perception.

The visual form of TV series contains two parts. The first part, the external form, that is, audience-user (change of communication mode) 4:3; 16:9; vertical screen image, and the narrative structure has also changed, from living room narrative to fragmented narrative; the second part, internal Form, internal and external situation and psychological factors are closely related, and form will determine the judgment standard of feeling. Although people's inner feelings determine the quality of a film and television work, the premise of an excellent film and television work is a good form, and on this basis, a good feeling effect will be produced. Film and television works are a creative form of visual art. Only by connecting with the audience's inner feelings through visual art form can they form the integrity of conveying emotions. The inner feeling will be presented through the outer expression, and the visual form is the transformation from the outer form to the inner form. [80]The refinement is as follows:

1. External form: audience-user (change of transmission mode) 4:3; 16:9; vertical screen image

In recent years, the vertical video (Vertical Video) format adapted to the vertical orientation of mobile phones has become the new normal, challenging the format standard and aesthetic taste of the traditional film and television industry's widescreen 4:3 or 16:9, and also reshaping the screen narrative strategy under different formats. The specifications of hardware devices have led to more and more videos beginning to use vertical screens. Many domestic mainstream media are also actively trying to adopt the vertical screen mode to carry out mainstream public opinion propaganda and political communication. For example, the App of the State Council has repeatedly adopted the method of vertical screen video + H5 to actively disseminate the policies of the party and the state. The

---

[79] Pan Kewu.On the Visual Form of TV Drama[J].Modern Communication-Journal of Communication University of China,2009(02):76-80.
[80] Qian Jiayu. Visual Psychology [M]. Shanghai: Xuelin Publishing House. 2006.1.

rapid development of vertical screen video meets the information needs and usage habits of mobile phone users. The data on the continuous increase in the time spent watching vertical-screen videos has shown that vertical-screen videos will be the main direction of video development on mobile phones in the future. With the awakening of "vertical-screen awareness" on more platforms, more products will be launched and become mobile phones The main types of videos viewed by end users. [81]In 2014, online movies began to move to the big screen on a large scale. According to the interpretation of scholars such as Yin Hong, "Internet Generation" movies mainly refer to the generation whose creators and audience groups have grown up in the Internet environment, and the creation, production, and promotion of movies all have a distinct Internet temperament. Looking at such films, we will find that they often lack a story with ups and downs and complete logic, and the usual binary structure and clear causal relationship are also broken, replaced by non-plot, "fragmented" and collage-style narratives. style. "Fragmentation" is one of the narrative strategies commonly used in postmodernist films, and it has become one of the most commonly used narrative modes in "Internet generation" films, including combined narrative, non-plot narrative, and open ending. [82]This refers to the change in the narrative style of TV dramas. Of course, this is also related to the change of the media and the development of technology. The change in the external expression of this visual form is mainly due to the public's self-adaptation and pursuit of modern life. This change is not only a breakthrough in technology, which enables us to receive and convey information more conveniently, but also just like the Gestalt psychology mentioned above, in the process of pursuing things, people will tend to The perfect psychological feeling, in order to satisfy people's demand for understanding things to be perfect, is the process of turning imperfection into perfection, that is, the process of changing the external form, and this process also satisfies the public's demands for diversity.

---

[81] Zhou Kui, Jin Luya. The Coming of the Vertical Screen Era: Research on the Frontiers and Trends of Short Video Types of Converged Media[J]. Television Research, 2018(06):11-14.

[82] Gu Guangxin. Collage and Irony: Narrative Strategies of Chinese Films under the Internet Culture [J]. Contemporary Film, 2015(11):147-149.

2. Inner form: form, psychology and motivation

The internal form of the TV drama's visual form is also constantly changing. The visual form is not a static existence, but with the changes of the times, culture, environment and people's psychological structure, the style of the visual form will also change. As far as the development and evolution of a single visual art itself is concerned, the transformation of visual form stems from such an opportunity: for art innovators, the old visual form language can no longer properly express what the artist wants to convey, so new ones must be developed. form of expression. Since the birth of TV drama art until now, the visual form has been constantly updated and developed, and the image style has undergone several obvious changes. First of all, technological progress (such as TV screens getting larger and higher resolution) provides the possibility to enrich the visual forms of TV dramas. Secondly, economic development, social changes, cultural shifts and changes in people's lifestyles make TV drama creators have to look for more and fresher visual forms to accurately express ideas and meanings. [83]This change of the inner form driven by the change of the outer form also occupies an important place. In terms of psychology, the internal visual form of TV dramas is the public's need for entertainment under the pressure of life or work to release their pressure. After understanding a change in public psychology, the creators of TV dramas made a series of innovations and changes to the internal form of TV dramas, which may be its content or the form of expression of the content. If psychology is the audience's requirement for the form of TV dramas, then motivation is a requirement for TV drama creators. As an art form, TV dramas not only show their own artistic value, but also have certain commercial value. Such a requirement also divides the creator's motives into four categories: one is that the motive lies in the simple and direct expression of artistic value; the other is that while expressing artistic value, it also requires rich commercial value; Value; Fourth, obtaining commercial value is a circular process in order to be able to obtain artistic value. Therefore, the quality of motivation also determines the internal form of TV dramas on the one hand.

---

[83] Liu Wen. Visual Form of TV Drama: From Object to Path[J]. China Television, 2018(01):51-56.

LAYERS OF IMAGES

An image is the material reproduction of human visual perception, and the attribute of any image is the image of something. An image is the material reproduction of human visual perception, and the attribute of any image is the image of something. There are many ways to express images in life. For example, the images reflected by mirrors and cameras are presented through electronic products. There are images displayed using electronic products, and there are also images created by subjective factors, such as paintings. Art. Images not only express the external image of things, but also endow the creators with thoughts and emotions, that is, creative ideas. The creators use images to construct visual communication, so as to achieve emotional resonance. The same is true for images in TV dramas and movies. The role of images in TV dramas and movies is to use the pictures in the plot to build a story system. The image expressions in film and television works are mechanically recorded, but also artificially processed and created. In film and television works, the purely mechanical recording of pictures by the camera is the most basic way of image expression. This is to show the objective laws of the image, and on this basis are the abstract expression factors artificially created. For example, the expression effect of images on static freeze-frame pictures, and the abstract concept in the process of dynamic pictures.

We can know that the first level of video is about recording, crossing the barriers of time, preserving the video you want to keep, and ensuring the synchronization of reality and recorded visual art works; the second level is about video Reprocessing, endowing it with a kind of aesthetics, plus the post-editing of the creator's subjective feelings. However, among them, the highest image level lies in the special abstract image processing of moving images. But as far as we are concerned, the image level can be subdivided into three parts, the first part is the reproduction level, the second part is the narrative level, and the third part is the symbolic level (symbol) image level, the level that restricts the visual expression of TV dramas,Aesthetic Value. details as follows:

1. reproduction level

Image is a camera's representation of objective things. The image in some film art works can be said to be a kind of scene reproduction, whether it is the whole narrative or just a part of reality, because it is also an image expression. But at the same time, it is not a complete image showing the real situation. The creator will add his own subjective feelings and considerations for the audience's acceptance when creating. Therefore, we can only say that the image is a part of the symbol of reality. There is the most intuitive way of seeing is what you think, and it also represents some different symbols that need to be interpreted deeply. [84]In the words of Jean Mitri, the function of the image is to reproduce the image of the object, "The image as a 'representation' does not represent any additional things, it is just a display." The first level of the image is performance here.

2. narrative level

Although the basic research object of video narrative research is the main body of the narrative, that is, the narrative text, at the same time, it is more about the composition elements of the video screen and the narrative language and techniques of the video. From the perspective of narratology, the layers maintain the development of the plot, and the low-level narrative is set up to answer the questions of high-level characters. As Genette said, the emergence of the lower level is "to satisfy the curiosity of these characters is false, and to satisfy the readers' curiosity is true", although all the technical settings of the entire episode are to satisfy the curiosity of the viewers, but his words are not without meaning. Reasonable. The function of narrative layering can be attributed to providing a plausible evidence for the narrative behavior, making the narrator's identity materialized, making people feel that he (she) seems to exist. The visual medium provides us with intuitive experience, and the lens is the narrator. Through camera cuts, the two levels of super-narrative and main-narrative appear alternately in the drama, and the plots of the same level go hand in hand and even influence

---

[84] Li Hengji, Yang Yuanyao. Selected Works on Foreign Film Theory/—Revised Edition [M]. Beijing: Life·Reading·Xinzhi Sanlian Bookstore, 2006.11.

each other. This is the cross-layer phenomenon. [85]This statement shows that one of the functions of images is narration, whether it is telling a story or describing a person, this is the most intuitive function of images. The behavior of how the image expresses the creator's intention is regarded as an interactive exchange process, a process in which the creator tells the story to the viewer through the screen. Constituent grammar, function and effect, temporal and spatial progress of images, and combination of sound and image. The narrative of TV dramas can express rational content through the recording of images, and the ideas of images are also displayed in the design of images.

3. Symbolic level (symbol) image level, level that restricts the visual expression of TV dramas, and aesthetic value

Movie images not only have the function of expression, but also have the function of conveying information and expressing thoughts. Image has a certain symbolic meaning and is a unique language. In Mitri's view, language is a means of expression based on symbols or symbols that replace certain things, and can organize, construct and convey ideological information in time. Each language system has its own unique characteristics. Film language is a means of expression based on the reproduction of reality, images and sounds with a certain symbolic nature, which can convey information and express ideas in the extension of time. Movie images are not conventional and habitual abstract symbols, but dynamic images full of vitality, and their symbolic meaning does not depend to a considerable extent on the objects or scenes presented by the images, but more on the visual background in which they are placed., The relationship between the front and back shots, this background relationship endows the image with temporary meaning. Cinema is "a language in which images play the role of speech and words by virtue of their symbolic and logical properties and their character as latent signs. An equivalence of perceiving the world no longer (in general) through abstract shapes but through the reproduction of concrete realities language

---

[85] Jing Yufang.Analyzing the Narrative Stratification of TV Dramas from "The Simpsons"[J].Contemporary Television,2014(07):76-77.

of things". [86]Some objective things in TV dramas can be endowed with a symbolic meaning according to creative needs, thereby enhancing the expressiveness of the image.

We say that the content presented on the screen has its own meaning, and it can also be said that it is the meaning of the screen itself, but the superficial meaning is far from enough for film and television works of art, and what it conveys must have its own meaning. The deep "meaning" behind the picture. The deep meaning is not presented on the surface of the screen, it needs to be combined with the audience's thinking. The meaning of the screen explanation is that the superficial and superficial can be transformed into visual language and conveyed to the audience. The deep theme and ideological connotation of the film are often hidden behind the screen. Symbolism is a technique often used in many films, such as metaphor montage in montage art. This kind of expression is not only the meaning of the picture itself, but it can trigger the audience's thinking and generate new associations. One kind of symbol is used to complement and express another thing, thus generating new meaning and connotation, which has a strong connection with the audience's self-understanding ability and cognitive level.

As an independent way of expression, image is not bound by any form or content. It is not a symbolic expression of any kind of thing. It only expresses the essence of things, but does not express any other meaning. It is only through the totality of facts to which it relates that an image has a specific meaning and "significance." It thus acquires a unique meaning, which in turn gives new meaning to the whole of which it is a part. However, it is necessary to clearly point out that although all images in a film are signified (through its content), not all images themselves have symbolic value, they are only incidental by means of implication relations prescribed by the actions they describe. have symbolic value.[87]

From the perspective of visual communication, the communication of art must be aesthetically processed on the basis of reality, so visual communication is the foundation, aesthetics is the way of art, and visual form is a special aesthetic. Excellent expressive images can strengthen

---

[86] Jin Hu. On Jean Mitri's Film Language Viewpoint[J]. Film Literature, 2014(07):54-56.
[87] Li Hengji, Yang Yuan. Selected Works on Foreign Film Theory—Revised Edition [M]. Beijing: Life·Reading·New Knowledge Joint Publishing, 2006.11.

the sense of form of TV dramas, increase the artistic appeal, and thus have a psychological effect on the audience in an aesthetic way. Only by understanding the characteristics and levels of images in dissemination can the artistic quality of TV dramas be improved. For the audience, only by understanding the characteristics and layers of the image can they establish a dialogue with the creator at the corresponding level.

When people appreciate visual works of art and receive and understand their meaning, they will also be influenced by prior consciousness and experiential knowledge, as well as the active participation of psychological gestalt function. In addition, the form of visual art is often affected by factors such as history, culture, society, environment, and technology. The study of "pure form" that uses phenomenological methods to suspend factors other than form has its theoretical value and certain value. Just like the heteronomous theory of visual form, the injection of all rationality and perception other than sensibility is an external manifestation of heteronomy. Therefore, the research on the visual form of TV dramas should build a composite knowledge structure composed of theoretical achievements from the fields of art, gestalt psychology, semiotics, and formal aesthetics.

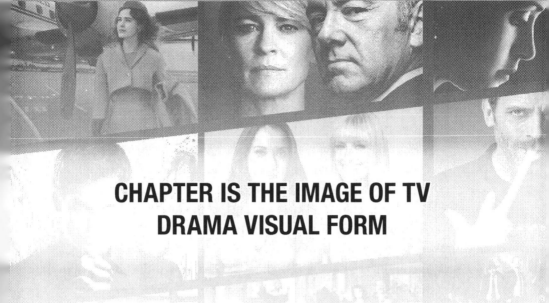

CHAPTER IS THE IMAGE OF TV DRAMA VISUAL FORM

The visual form of the image, that is, the visual form of the TV series, or what kind of image does the visual form appear in, and what characteristics does it have? According to Arnheim, each specific image is a form, and some forms are remembered by people, while others pass by in a flash and are not remembered by people. We know that the video narrative of TV dramas must be composed of a variety of images, some of which enhance the visual expression because of the uniqueness of the form, traditionally give the audience a strong visual aesthetic stimulation, and some images may not have a sense of form, but they are also indispensable. They reduce information uncertainty in a way that aesthetically redundant information exists. Here, we mainly discuss images with uncertainty, which attract the audience's visual initiative in a unique way, and directly grasp the abstraction of images in the process of visual thinking—this is often obtained due to the construction of visual forms.

(1) Image of structure

In a general sense, structure refers to the collocation and arrangement of the various components of a thing. The structure of a TV series is the way in which TV materials are collocated and arranged. The structure of TV films is mainly a collocation and arrangement in the time dimension. The arrangement of materials is a kind of combination of front and back, which is temporal and elapsed. The components of a TV series are diverse, including shots, sound, subtitles, etc. Therefore, it presents a multi-dimensional world.

The structure of the TV film is the means and form by which the creators endow the material with meaning and interpretation. A good creator should not only have good creative ideas, but the connotation and meaning he gives to the work is the living soul of a film. At the same time, how to use the charm of lens language to explain the creator's ideas is very important. The quality of a TV film and the depth of ideological significance depend not only on the content of the film, but also on the editing and combination of the content. The creativity of the editing team can play the role of icing on the cake, making the original good content more exciting, and some ordinary content can also be played better. On the contrary, if the editing combination lacks practical experience and creativity, it may ruin the original very good material and make the original wonderful content lose its due effect. The emphasis here is on the importance of post-production of TV shows, but the evaluation of good or bad TV shows is not limited to post-editing. Of course, the structure of a TV show is determined by the content. The complexity and changeability of life itself, the wide variety of writers and artists' understanding of life, aesthetic pursuit, and artistic taste will inevitably make the structure of TV dramas diverse and colorful. For example, the cross-reminiscence structure of multiple perspectives and multiple characters in the new era, the network structure of multiple clues interweaving, the candied haws-style series structure of connecting people or events, and the psychological structure beyond time and space, etc. wait. The artistic personality of TV dramas, the unique way of thinking and montage means of TV dramas provide the most powerful conditions for the ever-changing structural forms. The most basic and common structures are the following: one is the dramatic structure, also known as the traditional structure. It satisfies the appreciation psychology of people who like to read stories with beginning and end, and builds a balanced bridge between the appreciation subject and the appreciation object; the second is the prose structure, emphasizing the documentary of life and the authenticity of emotion, focusing on lyricism; the third is the psychological structure, this kind of structure has a jumping plot, fast rhythm, and large span, which can save space, expand capacity, show the intricacies of life, and reveal the spiritual journey of characters; ", breaking the limitation of the "fourth wall" in the stage play. It mobilizes the audience's sense of participation, further enhances the sense of reality and documentary, makes the audience feel friendly, and easily arouses association and thinking, fully embodying the unique advantages of TV dramas.

Knowing the structure of TV, we say that "morphological structure" refers to the external organization of the play, that is, the method of combining many stories in the future TV series. The division and connection, sequence and arrangement of stories; the proportion arrangement of basic structural elements such as beginning, development, climax and ending; determining the division and combination of scenes, etc. American film and television theorist Robert McKee divided the play structure into several parts in the form of diagrams in the book "Story-Material, Structure, Style and the Principles of Screenplay": a series of "actions" constitute "events"; Transform "events" into "scenes"; connect "scenes" with "scenes"; combine them into "acts" according to a certain "beat"; then connect "acts" into "story"; finally combine "story" into " drama".

1. Exercise

In a broad sense, people's cognition of things includes both static and dynamic aspects. As far as visual art is concerned, the transition from surface form to deep form is not static, but a dynamic process, and the medium and intermediate link that promotes its transformation is "force". We call this force motion. As the way things exist, movement is also a means of transitioning from the surface to the depth and simulating the real three-dimensional space in two-dimensional space. When we add the concept of sports to film and television works, it is not difficult to see that the essential meaning of sports still applies to film and television works.

As a dynamic visual art, TV drama not only has its unique personality, but also has the commonality of most visual art works. Works of visual art are based on objective things, coupled with subjective ideas. How to interpret the connotation of visual art works well, we cannot deny that this process is inseparable from the subjective consciousness of the audience, which includes personal social experience and aesthetic taste. But the most critical thing is the subjective idea of the creator, that is, something that the creator wants to convey to the audience. The visual form of graphic art is mainly expressed in pictures and paintings. Berenson notes: "Painting is an art that gives a lasting impression of artistic truth in only two dimensions. The painter, therefore, must consciously do what we all do unconsciously - construct his three-dimensionality. Also As Riegl once emphasized in "The Problem of Style": "All artistic activities begin with the impulse to imitate and directly reproduce the real appearance of natural things. Ancient humans wanted to present things as three-dimensional for the purpose of Make sure of it. "Compared with graphic art, video movement has added the dimension of time, which is an expansion of a visual form in multiple dimensions of time.

Dynamic visual art is a sublimation of static visual art. As Cao Hui said, "It is a combination of time and space. Every freeze frame of a dynamic picture is a static visual art work. In other words, Every movement of a static picture is a dynamic visual art work. Every dynamic film and television picture is completed by the combination of many moving or static different objects. The formation of simple visual power is not enough to fundamentally control the film and television picture The visual form expression in dynamic images should be based on visual principles, through the coordination and comparison of visual power among the various elements in the image, and create corresponding visual forms according to the different needs of plot expression. There are various ways of formal expression in dynamic images, but the common point of these formal expressions is that in the process of formal expression, visual principles are combined to arrange the dynamic visual power accordingly. Although the production of visual power has certain physical Attributes, but it is mainly determined by people's psychological reactions. The grasp of visual power in dynamic images must be based on different film and television creation themes and different plot expression needs to create a perfect visual form in the film and television screen in a reasonable distribution.

In the creation of TV dramas, video movement adds the dimension of time, which is an expansion of visual forms in multiple dimensions of time. Video movement includes camera movement, actor movement, comprehensive movement of actors and cameras, and editing to form a dynamic composition. First of all, the movement of the camera can record the state of the subject, and there is a real form in expressing the speed, time and space of the subject. Secondly, through the movement of the camera, the original static or dynamic things are represented, and the picture has a richer three-dimensional sense from multiple directions. Finally, the movement of the camera can also express the psychological state of the subject and endow it with expressiveness. To sum up, as Mr. Wang Weiguo said in his book "Into the TV Series - Wang Weiguo's Selected Works": "Camera movement narrative is to narrate and express emotions through the form of movement." Secondly, actor movement is After the actors receive the script, based on their understanding of the characters in the script, coupled with the director's requirements for the presentation of film and television works, the expression of the content of the script based on the feedback of the actor's subjective ideology. Then, the comprehensive movement of the actors and the camera is a process in which the camera and the actors cooperate with each other to capture each other. The cameraman and actors need to cooperate to fulfill the director's requirements, and complete their own tasks inside and outside the camera. Finally, there is editing movement, which is the process of reprocessing and recreating the formed dynamic composition. It is the creation of film and television works that rearrange and synthesize the dynamic image performances completed by actors in front of the camera to express the director's subjective consciousness and objective reality.

There are also many forms of expression in visual art. In the history of painting, realism and abstraction are the two main streams. After the invention of film, various genres of visual art such as realism, surrealism, and aestheticism coexisted and interpenetrated. However, TV art is dominated by the form of realism from the subject matter to the technique, which is determined by the characteristics of TV itself. TV dramas are not news documentaries, and cannot copy and copy life materials. TV artists use the external image of things to express the inner meaning of things through appropriate methods, so as to reproduce the reality of life instead of the material of life. The art of TV dramas is the use of image movement to transform static graphic art into a dynamic visual art form. Film and television works are completed in the form of dynamic vision. Although the principle of plane vision can simply explain the composition of each moment of the image in the form analysis, if the dynamic image is placed in a certain period of time for visual expression research, The original plane vision principle is no longer applicable. The visual power of dynamic images can be formed through the comparison of the moving speed, moving rhythm, moving direction, etc. of objects. The grasp of visual power in dynamic images depends on different themes of film and television creation, and the expression of different plots needs to create a perfect visual form in the film and television screen in a reasonable distribution.

2. Rhythm and its image expression

Catherine George wrote in one of his books: "Rhythm is to us what the ghost of "Hamletta" is to the guards at night, often incomprehensible and elusive. When we look for it, He doesn't show up, and when we're talking about other things, he's there—but fleetingly. The rhythm is charismatic in its very nature, but like a ghost, it doesn't come on call." From the side, it shows that rhythm is a dominant form just like the melody of music. At the same time, we give rhythm to the living body—generally speaking, rhythm is everywhere in our life, ranging from the cycle of seasons to the structure of human life characteristics. Every breath of the human body, every beat of the pulse, and every relaxation of the blood vessels are the powerful rhythm of life. Rhythm exists not only in the trivial daily life of the human body, but also in the spiritual and cultural life of the human body. When discussing rhythm as aesthetics, many scholars also attribute rhythm to aesthetics. For example, Yan Qianhai once confirmed this point of view in his book. According to his view, in a series of aesthetic or philosophical categories of Lao Tzu, Tao and image, existence and non-existence, emptiness and reality, taste and wonder, metaphysics and nature, these opposing concepts have been unified in Tao, which is the embodiment of a rhythm concept. And his statement comes from "Lao Tzu": "Everyone in the world knows that beauty is beautiful, but it is evil; everyone knows that good is good, but this is not good. Therefore, existence and non-existence are born together, difficulty and easy are complementary, long and short are the same, high and low are the same. Ying, the sound and sound harmonize, follow each other."

The rhythm in film and television culture also has its expressive power. As far as TV dramas are concerned, "The rhythm of TV dramas is based on the dramatic conflicts in the works and the emotional state of the characters, using various expressive techniques of TV art to form dynamic and static, dynamic and dynamic, static and static in montage sentences or montage paragraphs., fast and slow, long and short, strong and weak, etc., to produce an orderly "pulse" beat, and through the audience's physiological perception and then affect the audience's aesthetic emotion. In a TV series, rhythm is not Dispensable, it plays the role of 'breathing' and 'heartbeat' in the work." The rhythm of TV dramas includes narrative structure (plot rhythm, action rhythm, character change rhythm), picture rhythm and sound rhythm. Generally speaking, the narrative rhythm determines the picture rhythm and sound rhythm, and the picture rhythm and sound rhythm affect the rhythm of certain paragraphs. The formation of picture rhythm is inseparable from camera movement, picture composition, and montage theory, while the formation of sound rhythm is inseparable from sound, sound effects, music and other elements. Sound is also controlling the rhythm of TV dramas. The basic characteristics of the rhythm of the voice include the pitch of the voice, where music can be added, the length of dialogue lines, and the speed of speech, etc. The main goal pursued by TV dramas is to combine the rhythm of moving pictures with the rhythm of sound through the rhythm of montage, so as to achieve the organic unity of vision and hearing. From this point of view, sound effects may not be the main purpose of TV dramas, but they have undeniable The role of neglect. There is another kind of rhythm, Yan Qianhai called it "reverse sound-picture rhythm" in "The Art Form of TV Dramas" (the film and television industry has always had the theory of sound-picture counterpoint. The so-called opposition refers to the opposite of the picture in terms of rhythm and speed. Music, forming the complex rhythm and speed between visual image and auditory image. But after all, the opposition is borrowed from musical terms, which always reminds people of music and is quite incomprehensible to ordinary people. More importantly, sound and picture Counterpoint is not aimed at rhythm), that is, the rhythm of the three parts of sound, picture, and editing produces different degrees of difference. The use of "reverse sound and picture rhythm" has deepened the visual and auditory image of TV dramas.

If the rhythm of TV series is subdivided, it can be divided into the following four aspects:

First, the visual rhythm of the TV series. This visual rhythm is inseparable from basic elements such as light, composition, and color. The visual rhythm of TV is further divided into the rhythm of light in vision and the rhythm of movement in vision. Light makes us see this colorful world, makes us feel all the warmth and cold, makes us experience the ups and downs of life, and at the same time, creates the lens and picture of TV. Grasp the visual light and darkness, color and gray, depth and light, and you have already grasped part of the rhythm of the TV series.

Second, the plot rhythm of the TV series. "Plot, the word according to the current popular meaning, is the comprehensive arrangement of events in the story or things that have happened." Aristotle was the first to combine the rhythm of the plot with philosophical aesthetics so as to The person who expressed the relationship between the three. Therefore, the plot rhythm of the TV series not only affects the final direction of the plot but also grasps the psychology of the audience. If movies are a condensed summary of art, then TV dramas are a detailed description of life. From this simple definition, it requires that the plot rhythm of TV dramas pay more attention to details than the plot rhythm of movies, so that they can be more delicate. The performance of life-like elements. As the audience, what they value in the plot of the movie is the overall macro plot rhythm. On the contrary, they pay more attention to the "small plot" in the content of TV dramas. Movies can delete those secondary or dispensable plots, but TV dramas are different. It is those secondary plots in TV dramas that enrich the overall plot of TV dramas, thus constituting the main body of TV dramas.

Third, the emotional rhythm of the TV series. However, the emotional rhythm of TV dramas can be divided into three categories: one is the emotional expression of the characters in the play; the other is the emotional expression of the creative subject; Control the level that the public's aesthetic emotions can reach in a specific time period and in a specific situation, so as to obtain the unanimous approval of the aesthetic object. The first is the visual rhythm of the TV series. This visual rhythm is inseparable from basic elements such as light, composition, and color. The visual rhythm of TV is further divided into the rhythm of light in vision

96

and the rhythm of movement in vision. Light makes us see this colorful world, makes us feel all the warmth and cold, makes us experience the ups and downs of life, and at the same time, creates the lens and picture of TV. Grasp the visual light and darkness, color and gray, depth and light, and you have already grasped part of the rhythm of the TV series. The second is the plot rhythm of the TV series. "Plot, the word according to the current popular meaning, is the comprehensive arrangement of events in the story or things that have happened." Aristotle was the first to combine the rhythm of the plot with philosophical aesthetics so as to The person who expressed the relationship between the three. Therefore, the plot rhythm of the TV series not only affects the final direction of the plot but also grasps the psychology of the audience. If movies are a condensed summary of art, then TV dramas are a detailed description of life. From this simple definition, it requires that the plot rhythm of TV dramas pay more attention to details than the plot rhythm of movies, so that they can be more delicate. The performance of life-like elements. As the audience, what they value in the plot of the movie is the overall macro plot rhythm. On the contrary, they pay more attention to the "small plot" in the content of TV dramas. Movies can delete those secondary or dispensable plots, but TV dramas are different. It is those secondary plots in TV dramas that enrich the overall plot of TV dramas, thus constituting the main body of TV dramas. Another is the emotional rhythm of the TV series. However, the emotional rhythm of TV dramas can be divided into three categories: one is the emotional expression of the characters in the play; the other is the emotional expression of the creative subject; Control the level that the public's aesthetic emotions can reach in a specific time period and in a specific situation, so as to obtain the unanimous approval of the aesthetic object.

Fourth, the intellectual rhythm of TV dramas. According to the characteristics of TV, the role of the audience is the "passive" side, making movie watching a single passive behavior, but in fact it is not the case. The audience does not accept all the content of the TV. Not only "watching", but also thinking, which requires that TV dramas are no longer a reproduction of life, but that creators need to integrate intellectual elements into the overall creation. Modern psychology divides intelligence into general intelligence and special intelligence, crystalline intelligence and liquid intelligence, content intelligence, product intelligence and operational intelligence, component intelligence, experiential intelligence and situational intelligence, Gardner's eight intelligences (logic, language, Naturalism, Music, Space, Body Movement, Interpersonal, Inner), and Emotional Intelligence, which has become a mantra, etc. Intelligence in TV dramas refers to the fact that the characters in the drama not only have comprehensive intelligence, but also focus on a certain aspect of intelligence, such as intelligence in experience and situations., dialogue and other aspects of intellectual control.

How to control the development of the rhythm? For actors, the speed of the characters' movements, the speed of speech, and the change of emotions; Composition processing; for post-production, the use of synchronous sound, the combination of shots, the addition of sound, etc. are all very important. Of course, in film and television works, this is just a generalization of rhythm on a macro level. Grasping the rhythm of the rhythm can not only better shape the roles of the characters in the play, enrich the emotions of the characters, but also cause dramatic conflicts, promote the development of the plot, and make the film and television works more complete in front of the public. Music plays a role in exaggerating the atmosphere and enhancing emotional expression in TV drama works of art, and it is also an important element that constitutes the rhythm of TV dramas. In TV drama works of art, different types of music sound serve the storyline and thoughts and feelings of TV dramas. The overall tone of the storyline determines the choice of music sound, but the music sound also has a negative effect on the development of the plot. Compared with the visual form of art, the role of music in TV art works requires the audience to have a stronger self-understanding ability. The information of visual feedback is intuitive and specific, but the emotion of music is abstract, and the creator can influence it subtly. Certain information is conveyed to the audience, which requires the audience to think and perceive so as to communicate with the creator's thoughts. The influence of music on the rhythm of TV dramas is reflected in two aspects. The first point is that TV drama creators use music sound to convey reality or psychological feelings to adjust the rhythm of the plot. The second point is that TV drama works use music sound to express the psychological changes of characters in the play. To put it simply, we will form a fixed combination of music, pictures and emotions. It is impossible to use a soothing and warm tone as the background music for a tense and exciting martial arts scene. As Hu Zhifeng said: "The proper handling of music and sound can, on the one hand, accurately and layeredly reveal, reveal, and exaggerate the psychological fluctuations and fate changes of the characters in the play; The third is to overcome the limitations brought about by the stereotyped characters and environment in the screen, and supplement the fixed "real" part of the play, so that the inner sentiment and charm of the whole play are beautiful. The melody can reach an 'empty' state, which can greatly expand the artistic imagination of the audience."

The rhythm of a TV drama works is as big as the actors, and the use of music in the later stage, as small as the use of lighting props, all play a role that cannot be ignored in regulating the film and television works. The use of lighting occupies a very strong position in the art of TV dramas. The natural light effect shows a natural and more real scene; the dramatic light effect creates a fantasy and exciting atmosphere; when the two kinds of light When used together, there is a rich artistic world full of expressive flavor. The light of most film and television works is artificially processed or superimposed and recreated, but we cannot absolutely say that all artificially processed lights are dramatic light effects. This is the charm of light. How to deal with the effect of light depends on how our plot is going. In addition to the use of light, color can also affect people's subjective emotions. For example, red can remind people of blood and sacrifice, and at the same time, it can make people feel enthusiasm and warmth. Black can make people feel quiet, scary and lonely at the same time. Just like our TV series, it is impossible to directly hit the eyes and let the audience's emotions respond to the plot immediately. What the audience needs is a gradual process, and color plays the role of gradually giving people hints. "Color can be created in the The effect of people and objects in conflicting action, and changing rhythms allows colors to flow from one place to another, creating new and surprising effects when other colors collide or blend." Premise of Color It is light, which is a good illustration of the role of light. And how to grasp the rhythm of light also controls the rhythm of color very well.

Montage was originally a term derived from architecture, and gradually extended to film and television culture and lens language. According to

Professor Li Yulin, the word montage has a broad sense and a narrow sense. The narrow sense refers to the lens combination skills of film and television works. In the broad sense, montage is not only the combination skills mentioned in the narrow sense, but also the unique image of film and television. It refers to the expression of film and television images by writers; secondly, it is a method of layout of film and television works for narrative methods, space-time structures, etc.; then, it refers to the combination and combination relationship between pictures and sounds; finally, It is also the composition of the picture represented by the combination of shots. Therefore, we say that montage is an artistic technique for film and television to reflect reality and a unique thinking language for film and television.

As we know Eisenstein's montage theory: In Eisenstein's view, the meaning of montage is not only attributed to the selection and rhythmic organization and association, nor is it only attributed to the connection of plot elements. Eisenstein's montage theory holds that the juxtaposition of the two shots and their inner conflict will produce a third factor—an opportunity for ideological evaluation of the depicted things. That is, the new chemical reaction produced by the combination of separate montage paragraphs, the magical chemical reaction between paragraphs acts on the expressive function of things. Eisenstein summed up the function of montage as: "a logical and coherent narrative" that "can be as exciting as possible". Susan Lange said: "Once the rhythm is confirmed, it is implemented in the entire space of the film. It is born from the artist's original concept of 'allegory' and runs through the main part of the work... The whole act is a kind of The form of accumulation..." For the processing of rhythm, it can be completed in one montage paragraph, or in multiple montage paragraphs. Of course, each montage paragraph can be regarded as an independent individual, each individual montage paragraph bears its own rhythm, and each montage paragraph has its own narrative task, which is processed and processed to form a complete plot with mutual relations, with full rhythm. Even though each individual montage has its own emotional tone, it does not deviate from the theme. At the same time, we must also pay attention to the fact that combining the rhythms of several montage passages requires an accurate grasp of the inner emotional rhythms of the characters in the play. The emotional tone of the characters is based on the overall style, so that the montage can play a role.

When it comes to montage, it is natural to mention the long shot. The long shot is an artistic expression method that comprehensively uses the photographic means of "push, pull, shake, move, follow, rise, and fall" to record the whole process of scene scheduling. Long shot theory is also called "paragraph shot theory" which refers to a long, continuous shooting of a scene or a scene, so as to truly and completely express the thoughts of the objective world. The famous scholar Bazin has his own set of theories about long shots. He believes that the nature of movies is the restoration of the objective world. Dramatic omissions based on causality should be abandoned, and reality should be reproduced in a complete and natural way without cutting things off. time and space of occurrence. After the Second World War, French film critic André Bazin raised objections to the role of montage. He believed that montage imposed the director's point of view on the audience, limited the ambiguity of the film, and advocated the use of depth-of-field shots and scene scheduling. The continuous shooting of the long-shot film is considered to maintain the integrity of the plot space and the real time flow. Bazin believes that the time-space continuity expressed by long shots is an important means to ensure the realism of movies. Montage's method of decomposition and combination not only destroys the integrity and unity of the object world, simplifies and belittles the reality it depicts, but also draws the audience's attention to the things the director pays attention to. The objectivity of things is replaced by the director's subjectivity, and the complexity of meaning is replaced by unity. The audience cannot be in a position of free choice and independent judgment, the initiative of thinking and evaluation cannot be brought into play, and the room for imagination is lost. Therefore, he believes that reality is ambiguous, and only the use of long shots can provide the audience with the opportunity and right to freely choose the picture. Montage decomposes the complete time, space and events, which is extremely unreal. The director decomposes through montage, adding his own subjective consciousness, and does not allow the audience to choose, so he advocates canceling montage.

Speaking of Bazin's theory of montage and long shot, we have to mention Krakauer's theory: Krakauer extended Bazin's theory. Krakauer established a rigorous theoretical system in the book "The Nature of Film-The Restoration of Material Reality". His central theme is "The

Restoration of Material Reality", because he regards film as an extension of photography., whose entire function is to record and reveal the world around us, not to tell fictional stories. The purpose of his film research is to find out a development route that is most in line with the nature of film through the study of various films. To this end, he analyzed the materials and methods of films in detail, rejected all "non-film" forms and contents, and established his "film" standards. His conclusion is that only by taking a camera to discover and record those typical accidental events in real life can a film in line with the nature of the film be made. Krakauer is considered an important representative of Western realistic film theory, but he The rejection of traditional feature films has caused much controversy. In order to achieve the purpose of "restoration", he only allows films to play the two functions of "recording" and "revealing", and rejects all films designed by artists, with clear ideological intentions, and with a beginning and an end in the story structure. Even experimental films in purely audiovisual form are excluded because, in his opinion, such films tend to avoid telling stories, but they do so with little regard for the closeness of cinematic means, ignoring the intimacy of the camera. they have abolished the principles of the story in order to establish the principles of art, and in this "revolution" perhaps the art gains and the cinema nothing.

Some people call the long shot "montage inside the shot". It can be seen that montage and long shot are completely different creative concepts of separation and combination. Montage uses the division of time and space to achieve the purpose of storytelling, while long shot pursues It is the relative unity of time and space without any artificial explanation; the narrative nature of montage determines the director's self-expression in film art, and the long-shot record determines the director's self-elimination; montage theory emphasizes artificial skills outside the screen, while The long shot emphasizes the inherent original power of the picture; the montage shows the single meaning of things, which is distinctive and mandatory, while the long shot shows the multiple meanings of things, which is instantaneous and random; montage guides the audience to make choices, The long shot prompts the viewer to make a choice. For a long time, the art of montage has always been controversial. Many scholars believe that montage art puts the audience in a passive position, but the most essential difference between the long-shot theory and the montage theory is that the long-shot theory focuses on the audience's psychological real thoughts, allowing the audience to "freely choose their own views on things and events." explain". Looking at this issue from the standpoint of the audience, it is not difficult for us to see that the characteristics of long shots are to emphasize the ontological attributes and recording functions of movies, to emphasize the authenticity of life, and to belittle the role of formal elements such as plot structure and montage. Although the theory of long shots is highly respected, we cannot just obliterate the contribution of montage theory to film art. Just like Einstein's attitude towards the art of montage: "...the era when montage almost usurped the complete sovereignty in the realm of film expression is long gone. But many people are chasing prey and shouting to 'bury' montage This is also incorrect." (Eisenstein is referring here to the fact that while certain directors and theorists in the 1930s were concentrating on issues such as plot, character structure on screen, and performance creation in film, they In an arguable manner, it denies some of the artistic principles of the silent film masters of the 1920s, especially the montage as the main means of expression of film director art.

Although Bazin's long-shot theory has positive significance for emphasizing the authenticity of film and television works, it is too extreme to completely cancel montage. The practice of film and TV creation proves that both montage and long shot are needed, and should complement each other and develop together.

After understanding the use of montage and the theories of the two famous scholars, let's analyze the long-shot narrative. In the long-shot narrative, the creator often appears as an observer, keeping calm and objective, and strives to hide the creator's subjective tendency, including his pursuit of aesthetics and his desire for modeling, in the facts recorded objectively. Behind the images, an indirect form of expression is used to make the creation closer to the original appearance of real life, and to avoid the usual concentration and integration of materials in narrative montage. The long shot shows that the creator expresses his own understanding of the shot narrative under the synthesis of self-aesthetics, self-judgment, and self-pursuit. There are no high-level generalizations, no clips showing a neatly structured plot.

Secondly, the long-shot narrative content is rich and comprehensive. The long-shot narrative attaches great importance to the organic connection between the characters and the daily life environment. Many plots unfold in real life in the streets and alleys. There are many environmental shots, and there are often more procedural shots. What we can observe is that the use of long shots by creators in movies or TV dramas is mostly a long-term macroscopic performance of the environment, or shooting the state of the subject, or explaining the intention of the subject procedural long shot. Not only can it be truly reproduced, but at the same time, the audience can fully receive the creator's infection after seeing it through this narrative mode.

Then, the long shot is close to the perspective of ordinary people, adopts natural light effects, and pays attention to the recording of simultaneous sound, and strives to reproduce real life and real characters by maintaining the unity and continuation of time and space. Those modeling treatments that can make the audience aware of a certain artistic effect should be carefully avoided, and strive to be true and natural. What can move people the most is often the most real thing. Whether the long shot takes advantage of it or its uniqueness, it can bring the audience into the artistic effect it wants to express for a long time.

The narrative of the long shot, then, is a narrative that focuses on photography. Long shots use photography to complete the narrative, usually in the process of changing the shooting angle and adjusting the distance of the scene, using one lens to complete the tasks of a group of lenses in the montage narrative. Therefore, many expressions of ideas are conceived and realized in continuous photography. This requires the creator to use the feature of long-shot narrative after understanding the intention he wants to express, and to cooperate with the narrative of the shot to achieve a different filming without changing the angle and distance of other filming factors. Intermittent full narrative mode.

In the end, we all know that the narrative of long shots is an optional and open narrative. What the long lens records is an original ecology close to real life, and adopts a plain and simple photography technique, which gives the audience a sense of closeness and participation in life, so the audience may make their own creations based on the images provided on the screen. Evaluation and Conclusions.

In fact, generally speaking, the narrative of the long shot and the narrative of montage have the same parts, but also have different parts.

Just like the narrative of the long shot we mentioned above, montage also has its narrative method: the narrative of montage has creative The subjectivity of the author is to edit and recombine all my screen shots to what I want it to express; it is not as rich as a long shot, on the contrary, montage is a streamlined expression; and montage is artificially reproduced Formal expression, it does not have the requirements of long-shot and demanding reality, as long as it can express the creator's intention; if long-shot is a narrative that focuses on photography, then the biggest difference between montage is that it is a narrative that focuses on editing: Each shot is an independent part of it, there is no connection, and the process of establishing connection after editing. This is the different narrative expression of montage and long shot. We can see that montage pays attention to editing, combination and reproduction, while long shot focuses on reality and nature. But they also have the same identity. Whether we use montage or long shots, we aim to give the audience a sense of immersion that is close to reality when watching. We cannot say that montages are unreal, because long shots are also Through the expression after the design and mise-en-scène, the design itself is a kind of montage, so the two are consistent in themselves. We cannot deliberately emphasize long shots and ignore montage for the sake of reality, or demand montage for exaggerated and strong artistic expression without paying attention to the use of long shots. Effective use of the differences and identities between them will collide with different feelings.

(2) The right to judge by the audience (narrative ethics of long-shot)

The arrival of the era of visual culture marks the transformation and formation of a cultural form, and at the same time marks a change in the aesthetic activities of culture and art—traditional education turns to happy imagination brought by visual stimulation, and the aestheticization of daily life. The increasing diversification of visual culture makes culture a shared and art belongs to the public. The widespread dissemination of today's visual culture has made a new turn in the aesthetic world, and people's aesthetic psychology contains a new sensibility and visual novelty. The viewing pleasure of entertainment satisfies people's basic psychological needs at a lower level, and people's value needs will rise along a certain level. Modern social psychology research shows that "the pursuit of visual pleasure has become the basic needs of the modern public deeply influenced by visual culture". According to the aesthetic characteristics of "postmodernism", the aesthetic world will take a new turn: (1) The transformation of aesthetic subject and aesthetic object. With the permeation of commodity concepts, the boundaries between artists and the public are broken, as long as the public with visual perception ability is not limited by artistic accomplishment and cultural level, they can participate in aesthetic activities. (2) Changes in the way of aesthetics. Due to the qualitative change in the way people participate in works of art, there is also a contradiction between the two ways of concentrating and pastime in the aesthetic process of works of art. Concentration is an individual's worship or appreciation of a certain art category, while the way of pastime is often to form a habit first in the sense of touch, and then guide the vision, which is suitable for the public to accept non-worship art.

When the audience appreciates a work of art, the intuition that always participates in understanding activities and forms the basis of reasoning activities immediately becomes artistic perception, which is a direct, inexpressible and rational intuition. Both concrete and abstract, it is a natural light. This is one of the important characteristics of TV drama acceptance.

The visual form of TV dramas is a special system for the audience to perceive the relationship between various elements in TV dramas through vision, and it is the embodiment of abstract thinking in a certain art form in TV dramas. The visual form of TV series not only affects the creation of TV series, but also restricts the audience's acceptance and way of acceptance.

The audience, as the general public, has already formed a set of personal evaluations of the film even when watching the film, but there is an element of desire for the film to be easy to understand after all. As an entertainment activity to relieve the stress of daily life, what the public expects is emotional relaxation from movies. As a result, more and more filmmakers have abandoned the field of art films and turned to cultivate the barren hills of commercial films. However, if we blindly cater to or satisfy the audience's aesthetic taste, it is easy to produce a batch of poor quality films, which not only disrupts the healthy development of the thriving film market, but also confuses the audience's aesthetic consciousness. It will definitely hinder the progress of the Chinese film industry. The audience's expectation psychology is closely related to aesthetic needs, among which entertainment expectations, education needs, emotional transfer and experience are the most important aspects. Audiences hope to obtain spiritual pleasure and sensory satisfaction when appreciating film and television works. When you want to change your mood when you are sad and disappointed after studying and working, and when you are bored, you can enjoy the relaxed and free aesthetic experience brought by film and television works, and temporarily put aside the troubles of reality. People are eager to understand the outside world, obtain more information, and peep into other people's living conditions and inner secrets. However, with the development of society, there is less and less sincere communication between people, and the hearts become more and more separated. Due to the limitation of subjective and objective conditions, people's experience is limited. Therefore, film and television have become the best way for audiences to satisfy their curiosity and curiosity. Outside of work and life, people are eager to find an ideal spiritual world for emotional release, transfer and satisfaction. The art of film and television provides people with such an emotional space and spiritual realm. Whether the audience brings another side of themselves into their perception or brings their existing side into their emotions, it is all within the scope of the audience's self-acceptance.

Today's film and television companies, when promoting film and television works to the public, first think of who will accept it, how many people will accept it, and the scope of acceptance, and then think of the value of the work itself, but we must know that this kind of Value is also judged by the audience. This is also the right of visual art to the audience for criticism. Because in this visual culture, the focus of the audience is the critical acceptance of images. Just as Yan Qianhai said in "Film and Television Literary Criticism": "Film and television, as a technical means, pays special attention to the novel experience of the recipients. The audience not only weakens the patience of literary works to a certain extent, but also raises questions about the film. Higher requirements and nitpicking of traditional films have led to the emergence of different film aesthetic standards." Movies are like this, TV dramas are a daily existence, and audiences are constantly improving their self-aesthetics. At the same time, they also have stricter aesthetics for the art of TV dramas Require.

(3) Image landscape of TV dramas

Emphasis on body and simulacra

1. Landscape

Regarding the "cognition of the landscape", Guy Debord said in "The Society of the Spectacle": "The landscape has become a materialized world view, and its essence is nothing more than a society between people mediated by images." Relationship'" However, Guy Debord did not give a definition of the concept of landscape, and Tang Meng's "Narrative Theory and the Construction of Spectacle Society" believes that in "Perfect Separation", "the separation from every aspect of life Groups of images converge into a common river, so that the unity of life can no longer be reconstructed. Fragmentary views of reality that reconstruct themselves into new wholes can only be presented as a purely contemplative, isolated pseudo- The world." This passage became the basis for the generalization of landscape, and Guy Debo pointed out that "spectacle is not an insignificant decoration or supplement added to the real world, but is the unreal core of the real society." Here, the landscape becomes a kind of The impressive landscape created by the media. The transition from commodity society to spectacle society is a process of alienation in Guy Debord's view. He believes that the study of spectacle society should not be limited to commodities, but should be expanded to multiple concerns of history, politics and art. The separation between the spectacle society and the real society is not only because the power of consciousness affects the media's choice of narrative stories, but also the narrative angle and voice are different in nature. Narrative perspective refers to what kind of role I am, whether it is an observer or a person involved to express my understanding of events from different angles; narrative voice refers to that no matter what role or status I am as an event, what I express is support One's own voice or the voice of the opposing party, this voice can be expressed through images or directly or indirectly. When referring to landscape, we cannot help but mention narrative. From the narrative perspective, we know how the society of the spectacle is constructed: after the separation mentioned above, we can know that the society of the spectacle is false, and the society of the spectacle constructed by the media through the identity of the narrator actually expands the society of the spectacle and real life distance. And this also triggered Guy Debord's commodity authenticity shaped by video media.

As far as the spectacle is concerned, we can get a lot of information on the surface of society. The most important thing about how the media constructs the spectacle is to reveal how the spectacle society keeps the information of the real society secret and how to break the falsehood. The spectacle blinds the truth. It will make the society and the general public enter the hypocritical world with a beautiful and false coat.

In the field of film, Moore, a British film theorist, first paid attention to adding the concept of landscape to TV dramas and films. When it comes to the phenomenon of "spectacle" in movies, it is believed that spectacle is related to "the way of seeing that controls the image and pornography" in movies. Since then, spectacle films have gradually departed from narrative films and become a new form of film. The so-called spectacle refers to the images and pictures with strong visual appeal in the film, or the fantastic images and pictures created by various high-tech film means. According to Zhou Xian, the primary task of spectacle films is to convey visually appealing and enjoyable images through the combination of screens. Another feature of spectacle films is the "spectacle" itself. Spectacle makes films no longer succumb to other non visual requirements. In this article, I want to explain the two major parts of the spectacle image, the spectacle of the spectacle and the spectacle of speed: the spectacle of the spectacle refers to the scene with a unique scene, which includes the natural landscape and the virtual landscape. The natural landscape is the scene that can be photographed by a camera, that is, the original appearance of things. The function of spectacle is just as Sontag said when analyzing photography: "Looking means being in the things that people are familiar with and do not take for granted." The perception of beauty. Photographers are supposed to go beyond just seeing the world as it is, including what has already been recognized as spectacle. They want to create interest through new visual determination." Virtual landscapes, as the name suggests, are false unreality Landscape, when the creator expresses his creative intention and the real landscape cannot meet the demand, he needs to construct some special pictures. The constructed landscape is the virtual landscape; It is inseparable from the requirements of the development of the times. The rapid development of society makes people present everything offline to the public in a quick and concise way, so the creation mode of movies and TV shows is becoming more and more concise, which makes speed landscape a major feature of film and television works. The traditional film and TV drama narrative mode is no longer suitable for the visual requirements of contemporary audiences. "Look fast" and "Look fast" constitute the typical forms of speed spectacle.

However, the production of these two landscapes does not take into account the role played by the media in the middle. However, the medium is the basis for the production of the landscape. The speed landscape mentioned above is not only a response to the rapid development of the current era, but also a kind of capture of the speed of the object by the camera, and this capture relies on the power of the medium; In other words, both natural landscape and virtual landscape rely on the power of media, which plays a certain role in the recording and transmission process. We can collectively refer to these landscapes produced by media power as media landscape. The possibility of technology has driven the development of movies and TV dramas, and at the same time it has also driven the development of the landscape.

Landscape images include natural, designed, and image-produced landscapes—productive landscapes are obtained due to the acquisition, processing, and deformation of images. Borrowing Pan Kewu's classification definition of landscape, we say that landscape images are images in a general sense obtained through cameras, and become landscape images through the recording of landscapes, and this trend of landscapes has affected the process of TV dramas from production to broadcast. The landscape images of TV dramas include the following three levels: one is images. Video is the carrier of TV dramas in the entire visual communication. The video of TV dramas is a form of screen expression combined with camera screens produced on computers or other platforms. As Pan Kewu pointed out in the book "Mirror World": "The authenticity of TV dramas is based on the corresponding relationship between the images and the social life reflected in the TV dramas." But at the same time, the images and reality are not consistent, as Metz said: " We can see it, but we can't touch it, so we can't cross the two levels of the phenomenal world: the real part and the copying part." Through the operation of images, everything looks real, but the realism and non-realism of TV dramas are not based on This is what we discuss about the reality of images, that is, the reality of images is the unity of reality connected with the reality of the space environment, the reality of actors' performances, and the reality of lens scheduling and editing in line with life-like processing. The second is productive images.

The camera draws an asymptote to reality for human beings. However, media is not just a content carrier, but also a productive means. On the one hand, gatekeeping can change the quality and quantity of information by controlling the relevant links of communication, thereby changing the relationship between images and reality, and the audience lives in the second nature constructed by the media; on the other hand, digital technology makes visual images into imagination The signifier of the visual image can be both realism and surrealism, so the image becomes a virtual image. In short, it is a method of recreating images using media, which is a productive image. The third is imitation. In the words of Professor Pan Kewu, it is a simulated copy without the original, tending to a surreal world that has not been copied.

The significance of landscape to TV dramas already existed when human beings entered the so-called landscape society, and landscape became a separate aesthetic object: the display value of TV dramas is produced on the basis of landscape, and it is a kind of image display value with landscape characteristics. And when the landscape of TV dramas becomes a unique aesthetic, the audience's pursuit of landscape becomes a kind of self-awareness. Guy Debord, the inventor of landscape, embodies this in his photographic career.

(4) Visual form and aesthetic image creation of TV dramas

1. Traditional literary theory's cognition of imagery, Arnheim's cognition of imagery, they are somewhat close to each other in terms of symbols and nothingness
2. Visual form is a means of constructing symbols, such as giving symbolic meaning to images through the repetition of images, which makes TV dramas philosophical)

Hilde Brand believes that as far as art is concerned, the content of the work is not the main thing, and it does not belong to the category of art science:

"But sculpture and painting do not borrow poetic power from other arts. Nor is it merely to illustrate poetic themes. What the artist must endeavor to resolve is purely a matter of visual representation. The themes he chooses for representation need neither theoretical nor poetic significance. What he has to do It is to give these themes a unique and valuable aesthetic meaning. The reason why the beauty of art is higher than the beauty of reality is that it has been concentrated, generalized and typicalized by the artist, and injected with the artist's aesthetic thoughts. The beauty of art reflects reality Life reflects the beauty of reality, but it also reacts to real life, promoting the development and perfection of real beauty. TV drama works of art can make the audience feel emotionally excited, excited, and joyful about nature, society, and life. This is the sense of beauty. The art of TV drama is a new art with rapid development and wide spread, and it is the concentrated expression of the materialized aesthetic consciousness of modern society. TV drama is not only screen art and video art, but also a kind of social aesthetic consciousness and aesthetic construction.

Aesthetic imagery is created by the emotions of objects, events and their background. Pleasant objects, events and their backgrounds have potential aesthetic value, and act as a catalyst to stimulate the emotion of the subject, so that the subject can create it through imagination. As objective elements, objects, events and their background appeal to the senses, which is the premise of image creation and the basis of aesthetic activities. They are perceived by the subject as images in the eyes, that is, representations, through methods such as "viewing" and "taking". In the creation of imagery, objects, events and their backgrounds, as perceptual and intuitive fresh and vivid images, have the potential to stimulate the subject. In the creation of imagery, there are sympathy and tacit understanding, emotion and scene, meaning and image suddenly meet, and the subject makes a dynamic and emotional response after being stimulated. The objects, events and their backgrounds are generally fixed, while the subjective consciousness is rich and changeable, and there is a rich possibility of fusion between the two.

The replacement of textual aesthetics by visual aesthetics has become a prominent aesthetic cultural phenomenon in today's era. At the beginning of the last century, Benjamin keenly predicted the coming of this era. Benjamin believed that traditional literature is a kind of "narrative art", but what the industrial information age brings is an art that can be produced efficiently by means of modern technology and can be accepted "instantly". First of all, we believe that high Technology has become an important structural element of visual aesthetics. We perceive and think in the way and content provided to us by media or technology. Technology not only dominates our senses, but actually also dominates our evaluation system for grasping the outside world and self-examination. To a large extent, we It is through this method and content that its spiritual existence is realized. Whether we like it or not, technology today has become a big part of aesthetics. Secondly, "defamiliarization" has become the highlight of visual aesthetics. The so-called "defamiliarization", in short, refers to the creation of a novel aesthetic image that transcends the experience range and knowledge system of the viewer in aesthetic activities, thus bringing unprecedented freshness and psychological effects to it. Again, visuality becomes the basic principle of visual aesthetics. The so-called visuality, in short, is the relational behavior of seeing and being seen. Today we undoubtedly live in an era of visual culture, and visuality has become a cultural characteristic of our era, which determines our behavior and value standards. In today's aesthetic behavior, the visual dependence on the senses has become the basic reality of aesthetic activities. Intuition replaces reason, senses replace the brain, and the retreat of spiritual speculation makes us take the visual image that directly affects the senses as the first orientation of aesthetic value.

In Chinese aesthetics, imagery is the essence of art. In Arnheim's view, on the one hand, the image refers to the psychological image achieved by the interaction between visual perception and objective things; It is a real visual form when it is the essence of the image, that is, the achievement of the image is the result of the creation of the visual form. In a nutshell, imagery is mainly constructed by the abstract selection and visual processing from the whole to the part of the vision, and the germination activities of the meaning generated by the abstract selection and visual processing.

Taking TV as an aesthetic culture is because TV has aesthetic elements in its composition, and these aesthetic elements are the basis of TV as aesthetic culture. When we entered the field of TV culture, we actually entered a field of aesthetic culture. Television pictures are the main means of television communication, and as long as the pictures are presented, there must be strong or weak condensation and storage of aesthetic elements. The TV screen has its aesthetic expression in its lines, colors, tone, composition, picture combination, etc. The photographer uses these aesthetic elements to reflect his aesthetic feelings. Television is mainly characterized by visual communication, and visual communication is always vivid, vivid and specific, and the characteristics of communication affect the art of TV visual communication. The connotation of television communication is to disseminate all kinds of information, and at the same time, to mobilize the aesthetic elements of visual communication as much as possible, that is, to express with artistic symbols to obtain better communication effects.

The 1997 National Audience Sampling Survey showed that among the nine evaluations, the one that ranked first was "television enriches people's amateur cultural life and satisfies the people's spiritual needs." There is a broad domestic and even international market. With the progress of the times, people's requirements for TV are getting higher and higher. At the same time, the competition between TV and other media and the competition within the TV industry are also becoming more and more fierce. Emphasizing being close to the common people and life, we have to talk about the TV art style that is deeply loved by the audience - TV dramas. No matter what kind of story themes are, which dynasty it is about, with or without braids, whether it is farce, comedy, light comedy or drama, as long as it is well written, well shot, well acted, and close to the people, If the audience likes to hear and see it, the audience will applaud.

By analyzing the relationship between the visual form and the aesthetic imagery of TV dramas, it can be concluded that: First, the image depends on the abstract form. Kant believed that "vision without abstraction is called blindness, and abstraction without visual imagery is called emptiness". TV dramas narrate through specific images. If they stay on the surface of the images, the audience will only see the images. It is only through the abstract form in the mind that the image is truly perceived, the presence of an image is felt. Secondly, in visual cognition activities, the integrity of things is achieved through the relationship between form and thinking, to obtain visual communication beyond the effect of the picture, and to construct an image beyond the image. Thirdly, imagery is the ability to directly grasp the essence of things through vision. Therefore, visual form has not only become an important means of constructing aesthetic images of TV dramas, but also reveals the production of TV aesthetic culture. Even the production of artistic TV products cannot be like poets., writers, and artists can fully realize their personal aesthetic pursuits, regardless of the number of recipients. It is restricted by the nature of the media, the communication guidelines and policies of media organizations, and its production is not arbitrary. The background and interests of media organizations, whether political, commercial, religious, or other constraints, will inevitably have an impact on it. This kind of social group makes the production and production of TV aesthetic culture have a common paradigm, and the aesthetic individuality can be brought into play under the restriction of the common paradigm, which is undoubtedly limited. However, this social groupness also forms an irreplaceable advantage in its pursuit of social aesthetics. The aesthetic characteristics of TV culture are reflected in the style of art form, that is, its popularity. Popularity not only refers to the easy-to-understand content, but also suits the public's aesthetic taste and aesthetic level in terms of art form. At the same time, it must also take into account the nation's appreciation habits and aesthetic traditions. Popularity does not mean vulgarity, there is elegance in the vulgar, and there is vulgarity in the elegance, which should be the goal of the aesthetic re-creation of TV culture.

REFERENCES

1. Chinese part

[1]   Cao Hui. Gu Pengfei. Overview of Visual Forms [J]. Literary Review. 2006.

[2]   Cao Hui. The construction of visual form and the perfection of human psychology [J]. Journal of Henan Institute of Education (Philosophy and Social Science Edition), 2006 (4).

[3]   Cao Hui. Aesthetic Research on Visual Forms--A Study on Visual Forms Based on Western Visual Art [M]. Beijing: People's Publishing House, 2009.

[4]   Zeng Qingrui. Principles of TV Dramas [M]. Beijing: Communication University of China Press, 2007.

[5]   Cheng Wenguang. The Transformation of Visual Culture Form and the Aesthetic Demand of the Public[J]. Film Literature, 2009(09):10-11.

[6]   Ding Haiyan. Concept of TV Art [M]. Beijing: Beijing Broadcasting Institute Press, 1997.

[7]   Du Wei. Diderot's Aesthetic Thought from the View of "Beauty in Relationship" [D]. Shanghai Normal University, 2015.

[8]   Gao Jinsheng. Analysis on the Structure Types of Long-form TV Series [J]. China Television, 2004(01).

[9]   Gu Guangxin. Collage and Irony : Chinese Film Narrative Strategy under Internet Culture [J]. Contemporary Film, 2015(11): 147-149.

[10] He Yan. Analysis of the multi-dimensional influence of the new media ecology on the creation of TV dramas [J]. China Television, 2018 (06): 12-17.

[11] Hu Zhifeng. Outline of TV Aesthetics [M]. Beijing Broadcasting Institute Press, 2003.

[12] Jin Hu. On Jean Mitri's Film Language Viewpoint [J]. Film Literature, 2014(07):54-56.

[13] Jin Yuxi, Bu Yanfang. Multi-screen Interactive Strategy of TV Media in the Mobile Internet Era [J]. China Broadcasting and Television Science Journal, 2015(10):65-67.

[14] Jing Yufang. Analyzing the Narrative Stratification of TV Dramas from "The Simpsons" [J]. Contemporary Television, 2014(07): 76-77.

[15] Lei Meng. Warmth and Carnival: An Analysis of the Aesthetic Taste of Current Domestic Movie Audiences [J]. Film Literature, 2011(17): 22-23.

[16] Li Hengji, Yang Yuan. Selected Works on Foreign Film Theory— Revised Edition [M]. Beijing : Life·Reading·Xinzhi Sanlian Bookstore, 2006.11.

[17] Li Xingguo. Fundamentals of Photographic Composition [M]. Beijing: Beijing Broadcasting Institute Press, 1987, p. 141.

[18] Li Yan. Film Screen Composition and Visual Form Beauty Principles [J]. Film Literature, 2007(24):8-9.

[19] Li Yang. Strengthening the Aesthetic Function of TV Drama Art [J]. China Television, 1998(08):27-29.

[20] Liu Wen. Visual Form of TV Drama : From Object to Path [J]. China Television, 2018(01):51-56.

[21] Liu Yeyuan. TV Drama Art Theory [M]. Beijing: Peking University Press, 2005.

[22] Liu Ying. Looking at the Expectation Psychology of Film and Television Audiences from the Aesthetic Needs [J]. Film Literature, 2009(15): 11-12.

[23] Mao Conghu et al. History of European Philosophy [M]. Tianjin: Nankai University Press, 1985.

[24] Ni Xiangbao. Introduction to Film and Television Art [M]. Shanghai: Shanghai Literature and Art Publishing House, 2002.

[25] Ouyang Hongsheng. Television Art [M]. Beijing: Peking University Press, 2011.

[26] Pan Kewu. The acceptance of TV dramas from a visual perspective [J]. Modern Communication, 2012 (3).

[27] Pan Kewu. The abstraction and expression of TV pictures [J]. Modern Communication, 2005 (2).

[28] Pan Kewu. Mirror World·Visual Communication of TV Dramas [M]. Beijing: China Film Publishing House, 2010.

[29] Pan Kewu. On the Visual Form of TV Dramas [J]. Modern Communication - Journal of Communication University of China, 2009.

[30] Pan Kewu. On the landscape characteristics and significance of TV drama images [J]. Journal of Southwest University for Nationalities (Humanities and Social Sciences version), 2014.12.10

[31] Qian Jiayu. Visual Psychology [M]. Shanghai : Xuelin Publishing House. 2006.1.

[32] Qu Chunjing. A Comparative Study of Chinese and American TV Dramas [M]. Shanghai: Joint Publishing Shanghai Branch Publishing House, 2005.

[33] The application of visual art and aesthetic concepts in TV dramas [J]. Contemporary Television, 2002(01).

[34] Song Fangbin. The Formalist Thoughts of Riegl and Fauciyon and the Origin of "Visuality" [J]. Sichuan Drama, 2018. 6.

[35] Song Yongqin. Motion and Perceptual Characteristics of TV Screens [J]. Media Today, 2011 (7).

[36] Song Yongqin. Aesthetics of TV Drama Video Narrative [M]. Beijing: China Radio and Television Press, 2011.

[37] Sun Hongyu. The Fragmented Narrative Tendency of TV Documentaries under the Background of Media Convergence [J]. Film Review, 2014(18):86-87.

[38] Tang Meng. Narrative theory and the construction of spectacle society [J]. Southeast Communication, 2017.7.20.

[39] Tian Benxiang. Television as Aesthetic Culture [J]. Modern Communication, 1989(02):24-31.

[40] Tian Qi. A Brief Analysis of the Structure of TV Films [J]. China Television, 2010(05):82-83.

[41] Tu Yan. Dramatic Research on TV Drama [M]. Beijing: Communication University of China Press, 2011.

[42] Wan Xiaotan. The Meaning System and Aesthetic Presentation of TV Dramas in Mainland China [M]. Beijing: China Radio and Television Press, 2017.

[43] Wang Caiyong. Visual form autonomy and visual modernity [J]. Qiushi Academic Journal, 2014 (6).

[44] Wang Guiting. Outline of TV Art [M]. Shanghai: Xuelin Publishing House, 2008.

[45] Wang Nannan. Visual form expression in dynamic images [J]. Film Literature, 2008(19):31-32.

[46] Wang Weiguo. Aestheticization of Thought [M]. Beijing Broadcasting Institute Press, 2004.

[47] Wang Weiguo. Approaching TV Dramas - Wang Weiguo's Selected Works [M]. Beijing : China Film Publishing House, 2012.

[48] Wang Yanxia. On the History of Chinese TV Drama Creation [M]. Beijing: Communication University of China Press, 2015.

[49] Hildebrand. The Problem of Form [M]. Translated by Pan Yaochang and others. Hebei Fine Arts Publishing House, 1997.

[50] Xiang Huailin. Yin Wenqian. The Basic Trend of Visual Aesthetics from "Avatar" [J]. Sichuan Drama, 2010(06):66-68.

[51] Yan Qianhai. The Art Form of TV Dramas [M]. Shanghai: Fudan University Press (Professional Series of Radio and TV Directing), 2009.1.

[52] Yan Qianhai. Film and Television Literary Criticism [M]. Guangzhou: Huacheng Publishing House, 2016.2.

[53] Yao Li. Multiple Forms of TV Drama Structure in the New Era - TV Drama Research Series [J]. Film Literature, 1996(05):60-62.

[54] Yin Jie. Research on the art of blank space in Chinese film and television dramas [M]. Beijing : Communication University of China, 2009:6.

[55] Yu Minyi. Analysis of modality structure in contemporary visual communication design [J]. Sichuan Drama, 2018(04).

[56] Zhang Daqin. Being close to the audience is the way of survival of TV [J]. China Television, 2000 (S1): 4-5.

[57] Zhang Fengzhu. Chinese TV Literature and Art [M]. Beijing: Beijing Broadcasting Institute Press, 1999.

[58] Zhang Jian. The Life of Visual Forms [M]. Hangzhou: China Academy of Art Press. 2004.7.

[59] Zhang Jian. Artistic Will - Inheritance and Change, Wallinger and Rieger, New Art [J] , 2001, No. 2

[60] Zhang Jian. Creation of Visual Art Forms as Cognitive Activities—Konrad Federer and the Science of Modern German Art History. Xinmei Technique [J] , 2003.4.

[61] Zhang Pan. Aesthetic analysis of film and television blank spaces [J]. Film Literature, 2008(14): 24.

[62] Zhao Fengxiang, Wu Yehua, Xue Hua. Television Art Culture [M]. Beijing: China Radio and Television Press, 2002.

[63] Zhou Kui, Jin Luya. The Coming of the Vertical Screen Era : Research on the Frontiers and Trends of Short Video Types of Financial Media [J]. TV Research, 2018(06): 11-14.

[64] Zhou Yueliang, Han Junwei. TV Art Culture [M]. Beijing: Communication University of China Press, 2006.

[65] Zhu Zhirong. On the Creation of Aesthetic Imagery [J]. Academic Monthly, 2014,46(05):110-117.

[66] Zong Baihua. The Complete Works of Zong Baihua : Volume One [M]. Hefei : Anhui Education Press, 1994.

2. English part

[1] [Germany] Ernst Cassirer, The Logic of the Humanities [M], translated by Shen Hui, Hai Ping, Ye Zhou. Beijing: Renmin University of China Press, 1991. 110.

[2] [Germany] Georg Wilhelm Friedrich Hegel. Little Logic [M]. Shanghai People's Publishing House. 1817.

[3] [Germany] Rudolf Arnheim. Art and Visual Perception [M]. Translated by Teng Shouyao and Zhu Jiangyuan, Sichuan People's Publishing House, 1998, page 5 of the introduction.

[4] [Germany] Martin Heidegger. Lin Zhonglu. Sun Zhouxing, translated. Shanghai: Shanghai Translation Publishing House, 1997, p. 72.

[5]   [Germany] Martin Heidegger. Selected Works of Heidegger (Part 1) [M]. Translated by Sun Zhouxing. Shanghai Sanlian Publishing House, 1996.

[6]   【Method】Christian Metz, The Meaning of Movies [M]. Liu Senyao, translated. Nanjing: Jiangsu Education Press, 2005.

[7]   [France] Marcel Mardin. Translated by He Zhengan. Film Language [M]. Beijing: China Film Publishing, 1982.10.

[8]   [US] Rudolf Arnheim. Film as Art [M]. Beijing: China Film Publishing House, 2003, p. 2.

[9]   [US] Rudolf Arnheim. New Theory of Art Psychology [M]. Beijing: Commercial Press, 1996, p. 77.

[10] [US] Rudolf Arnheim. Art and Visual Perception [M]. Chengdu: Sichuan People's Publishing House, 1998.

[11] [US] Susan Lange. Liu Daji. Emotion and Form [M]. Fu Zhiqiang, Zhou Faxiang, translated. Beijing: China Social Sciences Press, 1986.8.

[12] 【Su】Eisenstein. On Montage [M]. Beijing: China Film Press, 1998.12.

[13] 【Su】Eisenstein. On Montage [M]. Beijing: China Film Press, 2003.

[14] [Su] Belinsky. Belinsky on Literature [M]. Liang Zhen, translated. New Literature and Art Publishing House. 1958.7.

[15] [Hungary] Bella Balazs. Film Aesthetics [M]. He Li, translated. Beijing: China Film Press, 2003, pp. 28, 29.

[16] 【Italian】Croce. Principles of Aesthetics [M]. Beijing: Foreign Literature Publishing House, 198.

[17] 【English】EH Gombrich. A Sense of Order—A Psychological Study of Decorative Art [J] . Yang Siliang, Xu Yiwei, translated. Zhejiang Photography Press, 1987, p.6.

[18] [English] Bell. Art [M]. Xue Hua, translated. Nanjing: Jiangsu Education Press, 2004.8.

[19] 【English】Clive Bell. Art [M]. Nanjing: Jiangsu Education Press, 2005, p.4.

[20] 【English】Lee Stowell, Commentary on the History of Modern Aesthetics [M]. Jiang Kongyang, translated. Shanghai Translation Publishing House, 1980. Pages 188-189.

[21] Color Film and Colored Films, Dreyer in Double Reflection[M], New York:Dutton,1973

[22] Encyclopedia Britannica Online. http://search.eb.com

[23] Sigrid Schade, Silke Wenke. Studien zur visuellen kultur – Einfuehrung in ein transdisziplinaeres Forschungsfeld [J] ., transcript Verlag Bielefeld, 2011. Quoted from Wang Caiyong. Visual form autonomy and visual modernity. Qiushi Academic Journal, 2014 (6).

[24] Concise Encyclopedia Britannica (Volume 9) [M]. Beijing: Encyclopedia of China Publishing House, 1986, p. 102.

This book has received funding from the "QING LAN Project" of universities in Jiangsu Province, and we would like to express our gratitude.

DONG CHAO, Associate Professor of Communication University of China, Nanjing and Doctor of Communication University of China, academic leader of Jiangsu Qinglan Project. Research interests: Social media, Theoretical Communication, international news, intelligent communication.
Email: dongchaocuc@163.com, contact number: 15950533376
ZHANG JIARU, Lecturer of Radio and Television College of Communication University of China, Nanjing. Member of Chinese University Film and Television Association and Editing Association. Research direction: Film science, radio and television art, new media communication.

Printed in the United States
by Baker & Taylor Publisher Services